La Conversation
Fracturée

La Conversation Fracturée

CONCEPTS OF RACE IN AMERICA

Clanton C.W. Dawson, Jr., Ph.D.

Rev. date: 08/06/2018

To order additional copies of this book, contact:
Xlibris
1-888-795-4274
www.Xlibris.com
Orders@Xlibris.com
768996

Acknowledgements

All projects of this type are social in character. While the construction of this work was personal and private, many people have contributed to my thinking about race. I first want to thank my wife, Maria Hughes Dawson who encouraged me to undertake this project. Thanks to my mentors and colleagues who honed the tools for the creation of a philosophical examination of this type: Drs. David Weddle, Joseph Bien, J. Alfred Smith, Sr., John McClendon, III, and Louis Colombo.

I am particularly grateful to the pastors and members of The Crossing Church of Columbia, MO and the Unitarian Church of Columbia, MO that gave me an opportunity to work out the theoretical ideas in this work with their members. I also want to thank the philosophy departments of Jacksonville University, Jacksonville, FL; Bethune Cookman University, Daytona Beach, FL; Colorado College, Colorado Springs, CO; Lincoln University, Jefferson City, MO; and The University of Detroit, Detroit, MI for providing academic settings to present my early examinations of race.

A very special thanks to Dick Dalton, PhD, for editing this project and providing helpful suggestions. Thanks to Valerie Berta for the photography for the book. Thanks to Xlibris Publishing for their help in making this idea a reality.

I am deeply grateful for the spiritual support of the members of Dawson Journeys Ministry, Columbia, MO; Mt. Calvary Baptist Church, Marshall, MO; and clergy and lay people who prayed for me. I also thank my students from Colorado College, Bethune Cookman University, Columbia College, and Moberly Area Community College for their support. I am most grateful to my parents, The Rev. Clanton C.W. Dawson, Sr. and Gladys Goldie Dawson who endured the worst experiences of racial hatred in their lifetimes, and yet stood proudly as African Americans. They taught me that there was a gift in me, and if I fed my gift, my gift would make room for me. This book is dedicated to them.

Table of Contents

Introduction

What is race? At first glance the answer to the question seems obvious. After all, we are constantly either engaged in conversations about race or, we are thinking about race. In the United States we are constantly confronted with racial images, conflicts about race, and racial issues. These experiences promote dialogue among us as we ponder race and racism. The more we enter into what Paul C. Taylor calls *race–talk*,[1] the more we realize that we are a society that is obsessed about race. As much as we think and talk about race, one would think that this society would be very fluent in meaningful *race–talk*, but we are not.

The cause of our inability to speak meaningfully about race in this society is because we are operating out of four main ideas or concepts about race that cause our dialogues about race to be contradictory and disjointed. While we assume that we are all thinking and speaking about what race is in the same manner, the assumption is unwarranted.

This project posits that all racial conversation in the United States is grounded in four main concepts: (1) race is a biological/genetic phenomenon; (2) race is a socially constructed idea and real; (3) race is a socially constructed concept, but not real; and (4) race is a matter of individual choice.

Where did the term originate, and what is it about racial dialogue that begs for clarity? History reveals that racial concepts, which decide the conversation and classification of race, have been part of a continuous anthropological, sociological, philosophical, and scientific inquiry in Western culture since the 1600s and perhaps before. Racial concepts are the overarching mental paradigms that guide our thinking about race.

It is suggested throughout this project that the four primary concepts of race at work in the contemporary era can be traced to our Western European heritage. The employment of racial concepts, as evidenced by our excessive racial thinking and talking, has influenced what and how we think of the world in which we live. Concepts of race affect our notions of citizenship, law, and justice. They influence our aesthetics and moral judgements as well as shaping our sense of what is sacred and profane. Our judicial and academic institutions respond to race, our customs reflect racial ideas, and our politics are obsessed by it. One needs to merely listen to a radio talk show, watch one of the many popular sit-coms or reality television episodes, compare BET to MTV, or sit at a coffee house to witness the veracity of the claim that race has unbelievably influenced Anglo-American culture. Talk about race is inescapable: It is all around us.

Each chapter will present one of the four prevailing concepts of race, with each concept trying to correct, refine, and/or eliminate the paradigmatic framework of the previously given concept of race. It should be noted that the focus of this work specifically addresses concepts of race within the context of the U.S. Our American thoughts about race are qualitatively different from other cultural and societal understandings of race. America has a unique racial history. Race is at the very core of the American experience. Sociologists Michael O. Emerson and Christian Smith state,

> For race is intimately tied to the American experience. It is what Swedish researcher Gunnar Myrdal called "an American Dilemma." Others have gone further describing it as indivisible from American life. Few subjects are as persistent, potentially emotionally explosive, or as troublesome as race in America.

Cultural, political, philosophical, and historical experiences and events all nurture these notions of race. They act as contributing forces to the formation of the concepts of race. Within the American context, the concepts of race are no different in this regard. As such, these racial concepts demand an examination if our understanding about the nature of race is to be valid.

The cultural, philosophical, socio-economic, political, historical, and scientific influences that have most impacted our concepts of race are grounded in a European context – first Spanish and then an English understanding. Even our materialistic notions of race (e.g. a classic Marxist class analysis) are heavily influenced by the western European ideas that prevailed during Spanish, Portuguese, and English colonialization and expansion. In _The Idea of Race_, Bernasconi and Lott write the following:

> Indeed, it is only by examining the forces–cultural, [philosophical], and political–that contributed to the formation of this concept, that one can begin to make sense of what would otherwise be its anomalous features. Nevertheless, the history of the concept of race is not widely known.[2]

Therefore, Chapter 1 will present the major forces that have affected our race thinking and _race–talk_ within Western culture.

It is obvious that discourse concerned with otherness and difference, grounded in race, has been part of the human condition since – perhaps – the beginning of human awareness of otherness and difference. While the term "race" is relatively new – given the length of human existence and language–something about different morphologies within the human species has always arrested our attention and imagination. If philosopher G.W.F. Hegel, in _Phenomenology of Spirit_ is correct about the subject-object relationship within the human experience, then pre-racial conceptualization has been part of the human experience from the moment human consciousness became aware of _this_ and _that_.[3] I posit that racial classifying is simply another form of articulating the phenomenological concreteness of the subject/object relationship.

Racial classifying is one endeavor – among many – to formulate a conceptual framework for understanding one necessary and important component of human otherness and difference. Given the nature of racial classification, race conceptualizing is both descriptive and prescriptive. It is descriptive as it engages in metaphysical delineation regarding the "other." Racial concepts attempt to describe the ontological or epistemic attributes of the "other." Racial concepts are prescriptive in that they determine for us the "how" of what we are to believe about otherness and difference. Given this prescriptive make-up of racial concepts, they serve as a normative category of understanding difference and otherness.

The way we think about race now is qualitatively different from how we thought about race fifty years ago, let alone one thousand years ago. And yet we think and speak about race as if race is real but act as if it is not. We are confused about the nature of race, and our racial concepts are in conflict.

Philosopher Paul C. Taylor, in his book _Race: A Philosophical Introduction_,[4] suggests that part of our problem is lodged in the nature of language. He offers an analysis of language in general and racial language in particular that I believe is helpful for understanding and formulating a rational concept of race. **First**, Taylor asserts that the utterances of racial concepts are, as with all language, ambient. We are immersed in racial language. Common ideas may shift in meaning from sub-culture to sub-culture and due to differences in geography, age group, and gender, but racial dialogue is inescapable. Taylor states,

> It has been one of the principle media of modern Western society and culture, insinuating itself into our ideas … It is both the condition and the consequence of the distinctive ways in which ideas get worked out on the soil of the United States.[5]

Second, Taylor suggests that racial language is expressive. In the first instance, _race-talk_ attempts to express some epistemological and/or metaphysical claim when employed by the user. In some ways, the racial language is a recapitulation of the Hegelian paradigm mentioned above. Race determination and identification expresses the "this-ness" of the subject (e.g. "I am Lakota.") or the "that-ness" of the object (e.g. "The only good Indian is a dead Indian."). To say, "I am Latino," is an attempt to express something that I know about myself and what I am. It is the articulation of a conscious awareness of Self and a proclamation of what I am not. Observe the following lines from Claude McKay's poem, "The Negro Tragedy," as he uses racial language to express his nature and the knowledge of it.

> It is the Negro's tragedy I feel
> Which binds me like a heavy iron chain,
> It is the Negro's wounds I want to heal
> Because I know the keenness of his pain.
> Only a thorn crowned Negro and no white
> Can penetrate into the Negro's ken,
> Or feel the thickness of the shroud of night
> Which hides and buries him from other men.[6]

The poem speaks of the pain and uniqueness of racial existence in a culture that observes, but never seems to understand.

McKay is expressing a) an awareness of a racial nature that has qualitative significance to his personal identity (i.e. Negro) and b) a racial cognition that fundamentally relays something of his self-assessment and the assessment of others ("no white can penetrate"). Racial language, whether prose or poetry, expresses two issues: 1) what essential or constructed racial qualities the speaker believes the racial subject in question possesses, and 2) an evaluation and status ranking of the racial qualities in question (superiority, inferiority, neutrality, etc.). It endeavors to express something about the Self.

Racial language also makes an effort to express something about the nature of others. When, in the 1960s, James Brown sang "*Say It Loud, I'm Black and I'm Proud*," he was not just expressing a concept about his sense of Self, he was also stating a quality about the other in the negative – I am not white, nor do I wish to be white. Racial designation is always the expression of "this" and "not that." The racial expression of "not that" need not always be pejorative (as in the case of Japanese versus Occidentals or Greeks versus barbarians), but expressive racializing is always intended to express an internalized realization of "not the other." Thus, racial language is, by definition, metaphorically expressive – it tries to articulate the distance between two subjects, objects, and/or states of affair.

Third, Taylor suggests that *race-talk* is descriptive of and defined by experience. It has the power to define and describe reality for the person as well as serve as a powerful tool for shaping experiences lived and encountered. The presence of stereotyping, racial profiling, and positive slogans and speeches serve as evidence of this fact. If language, in general, is the medium for taking the raw stuff of experience and transforming it into meaning, then the same is equally true for *race-talk*. Positively or negatively it has the power of describing real or imagined experiences in a significant way and its content is determined by lived experiences rightly or wrongly perceived.

Fourth, *race-talk*, according to Taylor, is intuitive – it suggests that the person knows more "about" race than the "what" of race. *Race-talk*ers know what they mean when they speak, even if they commit linguistic contradictions. The inability to articulate clearly does not prevent our racial speaking, it simply compels us to continue to speak, closing with the proverbial statement, "You know what I mean." In this way, *race-talk* is practical. Its intent is to easily convey the nitty-gritty of race. When one is called "Tio Taco" (the Spanish equivalent of "Uncle Tom"), every speaker of the language knows intuitively what is being asserted. When an African- American mumbles in speech to another African-American, other African Americans understand that trouble is near. Race language is intuitive and practical.

While Taylor's analysis is helpful, it lacks some key observations. Although racial language is ambient, it also can appear to be ambiguous. On this point Taylor seems to vacillate. The case below regarding racial language offers an excellent example.

When a person is called "bad," generally what is meant is that the person so called is of poor moral character, questionable ability, or something of the like. Yet, if I was to say that Allen Iverson, Leontyne Price, Colin Powell, or Michael Jackson is *bad*, most people would comprehend that I meant each of the persons mentioned are of exceptional ability and/or talent. If the hearer were to make such an inference, the hearer would be correct. The term (i.e. bad) would be used, but with a different meaning. The difference in meaning, within the scope of language, suggests the ambiguity of language in general and of racial language in particular.

One may say, "Well yes, some language uses may produce ambiguity, but racial language is of a different type. Racial language is specific and thus renders any geographical, age or class peculiarities inconsequential." But if that is true, what sense do we make of the following example? To call a person of African descent a "nigger" is generally considered derogatory. Yet, most contemporary hip-hop and urban poetry is replete with the use of the term "nigger" as an obsequious utterance. And in the contemporary scene we have individuals of various morphologies referring to each other as "nigger" (as in the slang, "That's my nigger.") as a term of endearment. Clearly what was being stated in the first case as derogatory is in the second case affirming. The ambiguity of racial language causes cognitive dysfunction and utter racial-categorical- confusion.

The result of *race-talk* is that we experience a conceptual muddle when it comes to dialogue about race and races. Taylor writes:

> All of this is to say: we can't talk about races until we get clear on what it means to use the word. Once we do that, then we can ask whether the things called races actually exist, and whether we'd be better off not talking about them even if they do exist, and so on. But we have to know what races are, what "race" means, what the core instances of our talk about races commits us to, before we can take up this question.[7]

And so, we will examine these forces that have qualitatively impacted the development of the concept(s) of race. Perhaps surveying the history of race and racializing will clarify what we mean when we say "race."

The function of the following survey of Kant, Herder, and Hegel in Chapter 1 is to note their influence on the contemporary problem of clarity regarding race thinking and *race-talk*ing. From this brief synopsis, one can see why the concept of race is so muddled. First, we see race is asserted as a natural variety (Kant). Next, we see race is denoted as an epistemic error that leads to a metaphysical horror (Herder). And finally, race is simply a natural kind with essential characteristics and qualities independent of our system of meaning

(Hegel). If the historical development shapes a concept, it is clear why we must still ask the question: What is race? Each of these ideas, and others, cause a confusion regarding the articulation of a clear and concise concept of race.

Toward a Definition of Race

Clearly, such a definition is initially problematic. To note some of the issues that will be addressed in the following chapters let me state a few at this point. We must ask if race is real or imagined. If it is real, what do we mean by real?

If race is false, why continue to talk as if it is real? Does race as a notion help us in some way? Some may argue that if race is a social construct, the distinctive traits and tendencies that the definition calls for may be only imagined traits and tendencies, given the cultural and historical context in question. Since it has been stated that *race-talk*, like language as a whole, is descriptive of real and imagined experience, what prevents the articulation of imagined traits in the constitution of race? Clearly, the historical overview points to the presence of imagined traits or qualities once believed. What guarantees do we have that such a phenomenon will not happen again with adopting such a definition?

Chapter 2 will start us on the quest for a definite concept of race by a presentation of the idea of racial essentialism. The journey will then take us through a discussion of race as a social construct with objective status in Chapter 3, racial skepticism in Chapter 4, and race as an existential process in Chapter 5.

My answer to "What is race?" is simple: examining the journey cannot be worse than what we have today. Perhaps the journey itself will reveal something cogent and teleologically instructive for the future.

Chapter 1

HISTORICAL REVIEW

Pre-Racial Conceptualizations

Humanity has wrestled with difference and otherness in the context of race since the earliest civilizations. The Egyptian _Book of Gates_, for example, seems to be one of the first written documents regarding the division of humanity into groups we now term as races.[8] The Book of Gates identifies four distinct groups, all categorized primarily by skin color. These groups were each described as having distinct physical, cultural, and custom differences and those differences in behavior were tangentially attributed to morphology.

Greek culture is notorious for articulating its concern and uneasiness with the phenomenon of difference and otherness. Aristotle classified those who did not speak Greek as "barbarians."[9] Herodotus is recorded as having spoken forcibly about not only different races, but also noting the alleged abominable sexual practices of the darker people of Mendes and other parts of Egypt.[10]

The Chinese attached great meaning to ancestry and appearance. In some 3rd century Chinese writings there is the complaint of foreign savages "who greatly resemble monkeys from whom they descend."[11] Their complaint included not only dark-skinned residents of Africa and South Asia, but also the "ash white"-skinned travelers of Europe. They were quite consistent in ascribing inferior status to both the black and white groups.

Israel, without question, saw themselves as the chosen people of Yahweh and practiced a strict ethnocentric prejudice grounded in their theology. Their chosenness was their badge of superiority. Anyone not a descendent of Abraham, Isaac, and Jacob was a Gentile. Gentiles were restricted from many customs and practices based on ethnic identity. Israel believed that only a Jew was an heir to the promise of God.

It is obvious that the Egyptians, Greeks, Chinese, and Jews participated and practiced strict ethno-centrism. I maintain that such ethnocentric thinking constitutes early **pre-racial** conceptualizing. It is ethnocentric thinking, but not yet racial conceptualizing in the strict sense. No developed systematic conception of race is present in this exercise of ethnocentric thinking. Race concepts need a scientific foundation (including social sciences) on which to stand and none was present at this point of human history. Only ethnocentric notions availed. By ethnocentric notions, I mean a type of thinking that categorizes one's own group – having a group identity generally based on color and/or practice – as culturally, intellectually, morally, and/or physically superior to all other groups.

It is in the Middle Ages that the classification of human groups in a more systematic fashion begins.[12] The Medieval models – of what we now call race – mixed classical Christian ideas of God's creation of humanity with the notion of human delineation. Resting on a theological foundation which asserted that the differences in morphology were due to the curse of Ham – or by divine design, Medieval thinkers asserted that humanity had descended from the sons of Noah: Shem, Ham, and Japheth. The result produced distinct racial groups: Semitic (Near Eastern/Asian), Hamitic (African), and Japhetic (European) peoples. None of these examples used the word "race" as a categorical designation of human otherness. However, one can see a **pre-racial** classification based on color and culture beginning to emerge. I suggest that this narrowing of classifications (Asian, African, and Caucasian) is the first real movement toward a serious concept of race.

The Emergence of Race as a Concept

Much scholarly debate has arisen over when and where the first concept of race – as we speak about race in the contemporary – was presented. Some scholars suggest that the concept arose with the Purity of Blood Statutes of 15[13] century Spain.[13] After Spain defeated the last Moorish stronghold off the Iberian Peninsula under the leadership of Ferdinand and Isabella, Moors and Jews were forced to convert to Christianity or face expulsion. Most Muslims and Jews did convert, but a tension remained concerning the new converts. The Spaniards were concerned that there existed an essential (racial) difference, carried in the blood of the *"conversos"* (Jewish converts) and *"moriscos"* (Muslim converts). This difference, claimed the Spaniards, was greater than culture or religiosity. Therefore, the Pure Blood Statutes were instituted. The Pure Blood Statutes gave power and privilege to "pure blood Spaniards" over those who Spain considered of mixed, un-pure blood heritage, and maintained the authority of the Roman Church in the socio-political arena.[14] Therefore, the Pure Blood Statutes were used against Jewish and Muslim converts to Christianity as a way of preserving racial and socio-economic purity within Spanish society. As a result of this social phenomenon, "raza" became a term that not only referred to breeds of horses, but also became a racial slur for people of Jewish and/or Muslim descent. Of this Spanish classification of people by physiological distinctions, Paul C. Taylor writes:

> Turning social and cultural difference into a physiological and heritable difference in "breed" – moving from culturally distinct peoples to essentially distinct *razas* – is the important semantic shift of the early racial project. This is less a new interpretation of race than the founding interpretation, introducing the *raza*-idea to examine social difference, and to depict difference and subordination as natural conditions. This naturalization of social status is, among other things, one of the key moments in the shift from anti-Judaism [and anti-Islam, my insert], a theological posture, to anti-Semitism [and anti-Black or Moorish], a race-based prejudice.[15]

This key semantic and ideological shift provides a telling employment of the first systematic conceptualizing of race that becomes socially codified. "Race" is transformed from a term for horses to a classification of people that is undergirded by the institutional church. It is notable that this shift also came during the time of Spanish (in particular) and European (in general) colonialization. While I believe the fundamental motivation of colonialization and slavery was economic, terminology was important psychologically for the dual continuation of slavery and colonialization. Terminology allowed the slave trading colonizing to be a more guilt-free enterprise, because the terms they used dehumanized the victims. If the victims are not totally human, then the ethical ramifications are no longer relevant for consideration.

The change from a theological classification of humanity (i.e. sons of Noah theory) to an anthropological theory of human otherness was an important paradigmatic shift. The movement toward an anthropological explanation allowed for a separation of humanity on quasi-scientific grounds. Difference of blood was denoted as the reason for the difference of human groups, not God's judgment against sin. The anthropological shift provided a basis for the later expeditions to the New World and the subsequent treatment of First Americans (North and South), as well as the equally engaged slave trade.[16]

> [Scholars] have sought the origin of the concept of race in the debates of sixteenth–century Spain when the opponents of Bartolome' de Las Casas justified the mistreatment of Native Americans on the grounds that they were not human. Others have sought it in the Atlantic slave trade. Clearly, along with the development of European imperialism and colonization around the world, the word *race* was introduced to the English language.[17]

The originating point for the use of the term "race" can be found in the etymological movement from Spain to the rest of Europe.[18] The term "raza" used in Spain "quickly spread," first finding its way into English and then into French. Francois Bernier is recognized as the first to use the term "race" in the modern sense.[19] In an essay Bernier wrote in 1684, he declared, "there are mostly four or five species or races of men so noticeably different from each other that they can serve as a justifiable basis for a new division of the Earth."[20] The "new division" followed the earlier models suggested by previous racialists. That is to say that the groups Bernier identified were: whites, blacks, Asians, and First Americans. What makes Bernier's assertion compelling is that it was the first time a scientific analysis of human traits (facial shape, skin color, and hair texture) was offered as a foundation for human classification.[21] It was the beginning of conceptual race formation. As I previously mentioned, a concept of race demands a scientific underpinning. Otherwise race thinking is merely "folk psychology."[22]

Bernier's work was also an attempt to answer the debate of the early Enlightenment. Influenced by Roman Catholic theology, the intellectual community was divided over monogenesis and its antagonist doctrine, polygenesis.[23] Monogenesis is the doctrine that all human creatures are the descendants of one ancestral family. The most notable form of the position is the theological doctrine of the family of Adam and Eve. With a monogenesis view, certain intellectual commitments arise.

> The first commitment is to monogenism, the view that all human races are varieties of a single species ... The second commitment is to environmentalism. This is the view that the differences between the varieties of humanity ... reflect the operations of climate and other influences over time. ... The last commitment of the monogenesis synthesis ... was to a kind of abstract humanism. The differences between human varieties were, after all, differences between *human* varieties, caused by the influence of external forces over time.[24]

The abstract humanism employed by the monogenesis camp (the notable exception of the period being the Society of Friends) was interestingly conjoined to a prevailing philosophical stance that the white variation of the human species was the superior human variety. A hierarchy of human variety begins to emerge as the dominant thinking in European-American culture. White variation was placed at the apex and, of course, black was at the nadir. Thomas Jefferson was an advocate of monogenesis, the notion of abstract humanism and the human hierarchy. He wrote:

> I advance it as a suspicion only, that the blacks whether originally a distinct race, or made distinct by time and circumstance, are inferior to the whites in the endowments of both body and mind. ... The unfortunate difference of color, and perhaps of faculty, is a powerful obstacle to the emancipation of these people.[25]

In contrast to monogenesis, polygenesis insisted that there must have existed multiple (four or more) origins of the human race. The multiple origins provided the *cause* for the differentiation within the human species. The general model was that the cradle of the black, white, and yellow races could be traced to the great geographical regions: blacks from Africa, whites from the Caucasus, and Asians from China/Mongolia. Polygenesis adherents agreed with the monogenesists that there existed a great variety within the community of human beings, and that the variety also is reflective of a hierarchy of talent, intellectual prowess, etc. The supporters of polygenesis suggested that for the diverse races to have descended from one species is a notion too simplistic to entertain. What is interesting is that the majority of both groups held to a belief that the world was approximately 6000 years old. Given this assumption, the polygenesists argued that external influences could not have caused the large differences in the people that were present in the world. What explanation could be given for the marked differences of the people encountered in these other regions? Only polygenesis, stated its advocates, was a reasonable explanation.

In 1655 Isaac de la Peyrere in his article "Prae-Adamitae" argued that there existed multiple Adams, one for each race, but that the first Adam was white.[26] While the intellectual community of his time heavily criticized his work, it was advocated by Voltaire in the 1700's and became a point of interest and response by Kant in 1775. More about the philosophical advocates and opponents will be addressed in the next section. Suffice it to say that Peyrere's work did not go unnoticed. Peyrere's idea also served as a foundation for ascribing qualities to human beings based on a notion of race, which was picked up by the philosophical community of the Late Enlightenment. My point in presenting this historical development of the concept of race is to prove the pre-philosophical influences that have greatly impacted our current thinking and dialogue about race. The following points bear noting:

1. Human classification moved from morphological identification to classifying humans along distinct physiological variations. Race starts to be the term for human sub-groups. Blood replaced color as the determining factor of group membership.
2. The method of classifying various races of the human species moved from theological to an anthropological and a scientific foundation. Nature replaced God as the cause of variety opening the door for scientific justification of variety. Science emerged as the primary tool for both discovery of racial facts and the justification of racial designations.
3. The identification of human races introduced questions of origin. Monogenesis came under severe attack as a reasonable explanation. Polygenesis acquired momentum as the philosophical position of the day. Along with the polygenetic stance came a ranking of races based on the natural tendencies of each group.

We turn our attention to philosophical discussions regarding race and races.

Philosophical Notions of Race 1: Kant

The German philosopher Immanuel Kant (1724-1804) is regarded as one of the key philosophical figures whose thought has significantly contributed to the concept of race. His epistemological rigor broke the ground for the consideration of race as a proper object of rational reflection. In 1775, Kant wrote the essay, "Of the Different Human Races." This essay significantly influenced the late German Enlightenment idea, and subsequently the Modern notion, of race.[27] Most commenters of this research project state that this work by Kant is "the first theory of race which really merits that name."[28]

Kant wrote this essay with two equal goals in mind. First, the idea of polygenesis, particularly due to the post-La Peyrere advocates, was growing in prominence within intellectual circles. Voltaire's _Philosophy of History_ had given polygenesis a philosophical foundation.[29] Henry Home and historian Lord Kames had equally supported the notion of multiple origins of the human species. The rising support of the polygenesis belief prompted Kant to refute its foundation in "Of the Different Species." Kant posits,

> In the animal kingdom, the natural division into genera and species based on the law of common propagation and the unity of genera is nothing other than the unity of reproductive power that is consistently operative within a specific collection of animals. ... A natural genus may, however, be distinguished from every artificial division. An artificial division is based upon classes and divides things up according to similarities ...[30]

Kant goes on to state,

> ... a natural division is based upon identifying distinct lines of descent that divide according to reproductive relations. The first of these creates an artificial system for memorization, the second a natural system for the understanding. The first has only the intent of bringing creatures under headings; the second has the intent of bringing them under laws.[31]

In the section named, _Of the Diversity of the Races in General_, Kant writes,

> According to this second way of thinking, all human beings anywhere on the earth belong to the same natural genus, ... even if we find great dissimilarities in their form. ... More specifically, we must ... assume that all human beings belong to the one line of descent from which ... they emerged, or from which they might at least possibly have emerged.[32]

Kant provides a "clear and consistent terminological distinction between race (i.e. human) and species ... which neither his ideological opponents nor those who concurred with Kant philosophically had done."[33]

The second concern for Kant was how the plethora of information that was bombarding Europe regarding other peoples and their distinct customs should be organized in a systematic manner. Kant's theory of race provided an answer to the question.

> Among the deviations, that is, among the hereditary dissimilarities that we find in animals that belong to a single line of descent, are those called races. Races are deviations that are constantly preserved over generations and come about as a consequence of migration (dislocation to other regions) or through interbreeding with other deviations of the same line of descent, which always produces half-breed off-spring.
>
> ... Negroes and whites are clearly not different species of human beings (since they presumably belong to one line of descent), but they do comprise two different races.[34]

Kant goes on to suggest the following:

> I believe that we only need to assume four races in order to be able to derive all of the enduring distinctions immediately recognizable within the human genus. They are: (1) the white race; (2) the Negro race; (3) the Hun race (Mongol or Kalmuck); and (4) the Hindu or Hindustani race.

> Human beings were created in such a way that they might live in every climate and endure each and every condition of the land. Consequently, numerous seeds and natural predispositions must lie ready in human beings ... These seeds and natural predispositions appear to be inborn This is to say that they could be the factors responsible for establishing race.[35]

From the above it appears that Kant's argument flows in the following way.

1) All human beings descend from one ancestral line of origin.
2) Given 1), all humans share the same genus and species.
3) Races are distinct variations of the same species, and the variety is not indicative of different species.
4) The predispositions for race lie within human beings (inborn) and are caused to actualize by both internal and external factors including environmental ones.
5) Racial characteristics are the actualization of racial predispositions in human beings.
6) Racial variations and the subsequent characteristics are essential to the human being.

Kant must be given credit for attempting to provide us with the first rigorous scientific examination of the concept of race. In spite of his limited scientific knowledge (as compared to a 21st century scientific understanding), Kant's theory of race served as a commencement for a serious thought about race. Tommy L. Lott speaks of the issue of Kant's day.

> It seemed that if environment [alone] accounted for the races, then whites who moved to America or Africa would, after a number of generations, take on the characteristics of Native Americans and Africans. Any evidence to the contrary was hard to reconcile for monogenesis. By arguing that the original human beings carried the seeds of all four races, that one of those seeds was actualized by environmental conditions, and that there could neither be a reversion to the original stem nor a change to another race, Kant provided an alternative explanation.[36]

The problem with Kant's analysis is two-fold. First, it attempts to naturalize social difference. In doing so, morphology and other racial characteristics (shape of eyes, height, hair texture to name a few) become essential characteristics of the subject. But what is the evidence that such qualities are a) essential and b) predispositional? More about this will be addressed in Chapter 2, but the question remains relevant. One could easily argue that race is merely a social construct and the essential predispositions Kant purports are fallacious. Since one of the negative consequences of otherness and difference is subjugation, it is easy to see how, given the Kantian racialism, that the racial characteristics of non-Europeans (or of any group for that matter) can be used as license to invoke signs of inferiority. Paul C. Taylor pens,

> On the theoretical level this meant dividing humankind into deeply distinct but still related varieties. On the practical level it meant turning social and cultural differences into elaborate and far-reaching relations of privilege and domination. It theorized and therefore widened the gap between races, treating them not as provisionally differentiated varieties but as essentially distinct types.[37]

The Kantian model was easily turned into "a mechanism for racial domination and the mechanisms for disseminating the new racial "knowledge."

The second problem with the Kantian model is that it operates by a false biological model. Again, more about this will be contended with in Chapter 4, but clearly human beings, since our origination in Kenya, are so intermingled that "lines of descent would be hard to outline.[38] This is not an attack on Kant per se, for he could only use the scientific data available at the time. However, the current debates in genetics suggest to us that the metaphysical assumption the Kantian model uses just does not seem plausible. Again, this issue will be further addressed in Chapter 4.

Kant is the progenitor of a modern racialism that has adherents in the contemporary. Racialism is a body of knowledge concerning the nature of race. Kant's theory of race utilizes a racialism that is consistent with a Modern view. Thus, Kant must be mentioned in this historical overview if we are to rightly make sense of the current intellectual muddle regarding a concept of race. His contribution is significant.

Philosophical Notions of Race 2: Herder

As much as Kant insisted that a rigorous scientific concept of race was necessary, German philosopher of history, Johan Gottfried von Herder (1744-1803) was as equally opposed. In his *Ideas on the Philosophy of the History of Humankind*, though once a student of Kant, he rejects Kant's theory of race because it transformed humanity into "human monsters and deformities" contrary to nature.[39] Herder believed that every nation (i.e. people) contributed to humanity and that the nature of a nation (a people) was expressed through its *volksgeist,* the unchanging spirit of a people through history. In his classical unsystematic style, Herder writes:

> ... each human being in the end becomes a world, that may have a similar appearance from the outside; but on the inside has a nature of its own that cannot be measured against any other. ... The whole course of a human being's life is transformation; all of the stages of his life are fables on it and hence the whole of humankind is engaged in a continuing metamorphosis. ... And so human history becomes a theater of transformations ... Since however the human intellect seeks unity through all of this differentiation, and its model, the divine intellect, has married unity with the innumerable diversity on earth, we can therefore return here once again from the colossal domain of changes back to the simplest statement: only *One and the same species is humankind on earth.*[40]

Herder goes on to say about those who reject Kant's theory of race and his supporters:

> How many ancient fables about human monsters and deformities have already been lost through the light of history! ... Men who succeed in banishing mistakes from creation, lies from our memory, and insults from our nature are to the realm of truth just what the heroes in the fables were to the first world; they reduce the number of monsters on earth.[41]

From these excerpts we get a sense of Herder's argument against Kant. Herder objects to categorizing humanity into races. Herder suggests that when we think in terms of race, we commit an epistemological error that results in metaphysical horror. In so defining the human community in terms of races (the epistemological error), we "deform" people, and thus the whole of humanity by turning human beings into sub-humans and monstrous things[42] (the metaphysical horror).

> Neither the pongo nor the gibbon is your brother, whereas the American and the Negro certainly are. You should not oppress him, nor murder him, nor steal from him: for he is a human being just as you are. You may not enter into fraternity with the apes.[43]

Rather, we should think of humanity as "peoples" or "nations" each developing, transforming, and moving toward the actualization of their goal as a people. Thus, an individual people's development contributes to the overall development of the human community. Each people have something of importance to contribute. Herder concludes by writing the following.

> Finally, I would not like the distinctions that have been interjected into humankind out of a laudable zeal for a comprehensive science to be extended beyond their legitimate boundaries. Some have for example ventured to call four or five divisions among humans, which were originally constructed according to regions or even according to colors, *races*; I see no reason for this name. … For each people is a people: it has its national culture and its language; … but it has not destroyed the original ancestral core construction of the nation. … In short, there are neither four nor five races, nor are there exclusive varieties on earth. The colors run into one another; the cultures serve the genetic character; and overall and in the end everything is only a shade of one and the same great portrait that extends across all the spaces and times of the earth. It belongs less to the systematic history of nature than to the physical-geographic history of humanity.[44]

Herder's influence on the concept of race is without question. Many scholars tie his idea about people and culture to the formation of National Socialism in Germany and the later Nazism.[45] Other thinkers, though diametrically opposite to the racism of Nazism, have imported Herder's thought. Names such as W.E.B. Du Bois, Zapata of the Mexican Liberation, Martin Luther King, Jr., and Gustavo Gutierrez all echo Herder's fundamental claims. These notable proponents agree that a peoples' culture and language help shape the total human spectrum and assert with Herder that each have a mandate to contribute to the human ideal. Yet, Herder's denial of race – on epistemological grounds – caused him to lose favor in the years after the publication of *Ideas on the Philosophy of the History of Humankind.* It was due to: 1) Kant's emergence as the premier philosopher of the age and 2) the scientific support of Kant by Johann Friedrich Blumenbach. Blumenbach's work, *On the Natural Variety of Mankind,* published the same year as Kant's "Of the Different Human Races," undergirded Kant's theory of race on physico-mechanical and teleological grounds.[46]

Bernasconi and Lott write,

> [I]t was clear that Herder had, at least for the time being, lost the argument. Because the first edition of Blumenbach's great work, *On the Natural Variety of Mankind,* was published in 1775, the same year Kant's first essay on race, and because Blumenbach himself directly engaged in scientific research, it is sometimes suggested that Blumenbach introduced the scientific concept of race at the same time that Kant did. However, it was only in 1795 in the third edition of this work, seemingly under Kant's influence, that Blumenbach recognized that his own great innovation, the idea of formative force (*Bildungstrieb),* gave him a basis for an enriched discussion of degeneration [of races] ... Blumenbach's varieties were thereby not merely a matter of description. Rather, they were part of what Kant had called "natural history."[47]

Herder's concept of peoples' capacity to fulfill their historical mission has in the contemporary period been joined with a concept of socio-historical racial essence. It has become the motivation for multiculturalism. The question is, Can such an essence be demonstrated? The subsequent chapters will each tackle this question both for and against the notion of racial essence. However, the historical overview at this point has provided us with the rudimentary formation of the problem. We shall look at one more philosopher to complete the picture.

Philosophical Notions of Race 3: Hegel

In a truly dialectical fashion, Georg Wilhelm Friedrich Hegel (1770-1831) gives the consummating synthesis of a 19th century concept of race. Hegel's philosophy of history attempted to resolve the problems of both Kant and Herder. Hegel insisted that the decisive historical category was not race but people (*Volk*). Races simply have a structural role in the unfolding of Absolute Spirit in history. World history, maintained Hegel, began with the Caucasian race, with all other races having a provisional role. Only the African (Negro) race had no role at all. Hegel, responding to the genesis question, states in "Anthropology,"

> With respect to the diversity of races of mankind it must be remembered first of all that the purely historical question, whether all these races sprang from a single pair of human beings or from several, is of no concern whatever to us in philosophy. Importance was attached to this question because it was believed that by assuming descent from several couples, the mental or spiritual superiority of one race over another could be explained, ... But descent affords no ground for granting or denying freedom and dominion to human beings. Man is implicitly rational; herein lies the possibility of equal justice for all men ....[48]

However, Hegel goes on to assert,

> The difference between the races of mankind is still a natural difference, that is, a difference which, in the first instance, concerns the natural soul. As such, the difference is connected with the geographical differences to those parts of the world where human beings are gathered

together in masses. … In these organic divisions of the Earth's individuality there is an element of necessity, the detailed exposition of which belongs to geography.[49]

From Hegel we can conclude that the difference between races is a natural one, evidenced by geography. Since all people are rational, may we thus conclude that we are therefore all equal as natural souls? To this Hegel says no.

[W]e shall now characterize the racial diversities of humanity in their … mental or spiritual bearings which go together with these differences. … The mental and spiritual characteristics of these races are as follows. Negroes are to be regarded as a race of children who remain immersed in their state of uninterested naiveté'. They are sold, and let themselves be sold, without any reflection on the rights or wrongs of the matter. The Higher which they feel they do not hold fast to, it is only a fugitive thought. This higher they transfer to the first stone they come across, thus making it their fetish and they throw this fetish away if it fails to help them. Good natured and harmless when at peace, they can become suddenly enraged and then commit the most frightful cruelties. … [T]hey do not attain to the feeling of human personality, their mentality is quite dormant, remaining sunk within itself and making no progress, and thus corresponding to the compact, differenceless mass of the African continent.[50]

Of Asians (Mongols), Hegel states, "The Mongols, on the other hand, rise above the childish naiveté; they reveal as their characteristic feature a restless mobility which comes to no fixed result and impels them to spread like monstrous locust swarms over other countries and then sink back again into the thoughtless indifference and dull inertia …." What then is the natural soul that is the crown of humanity?

It is the Caucasian race that mind first attains to absolute unity with itself. Here for the first time, mind enters into complete opposition to the life of Nature, apprehends itself in its absolute self-dependence, wrests itself free from the fluctuation between one extreme and the other, achieves self-determination, self-development, and in doing so creates world history. ... This advance is first brought about by the Caucasian race.[51]

Hegel presents us with the following conclusions:

1) While all humans are rational beings, there are differences in humanity that are necessary differences, not contingent ones.
2) These differences are caused by the instantiation of Absolute Spirit in particular geo-historical moments, called continents.
3) Each race particular to the continents possesses different stages of natural soul development: Caucasians at the zenith, African at the nadir.
4) Therefore, each race's provisional role in the contribution to world history is determined by their place in the hierarchy of races.

What Hegel accomplishes in his philosophy of history is a unique synthesis of Kant's concept of race with Herder's notion of people. Kant's cosmopolitanism is sacrificed in order to maintain the prominence of the Caucasian race. Simultaneously, Hegel is able to affirm both universal human equality, and racial superiority. The hierarchy of races is grounded not in social structure nor origin of humanity. Instead, racial difference is a kind of "naturalism," such that race has a particular nature, like other items of nature (e.g. whales, trees, birds, etc.). The essential nature of race is definable and observable. This Hegelian notion of race stands over and against a social constructionist concept of race that presumes that race is something human societies have constructed. Taylor defines social constructionism and racial naturalism in the following manner.

> Different cultures, in different places and times, have different conceptions of race – which is to say that each may have its own complement of racial groups. Many people take this to show that races are socially constructed, that we create racial categories and sort ourselves into them.... On this view race becomes an element in a discourse, a discourse, as it happens, of human social difference and

biological variation. Social constructionism arose as a reaction to the [Hegelian] view that races are natural kinds, that, like rocks and quasars, races are naturally occurring elements of a universe that is, in its arrangement and constitution, utterly indifferent to our systems of meaning.[52]

What the Hegelian notion of race contributes to the overall concept of race is the preliminary idea of a racial naturalism that is present in the contemporary arena. Racial naturalism easily lends itself to an essentialism that ranks races in positions of superiority. We shall see whether this type of racial classification is valid or invalid. The ensuing chapters will each make a case for or against racial classification of this kind. Suffice it for now to note that such a naturalistic essentialism has historical roots in Hegel.

Chapter 2

RACIAL ESSENTIALISM OR RACE AS A BIOLOGICAL/GENETIC PHENOMENON

Human beings have engaged in race conceptualizing or racial thinking for a very long time. History proves that we have thought about race since the institution of The Pure Blood Statutes in Spain in the 15th century. In fact, it was during this time in Spanish history that the term race (raza) appeared. Previously the term referred to diseased or substandard animals. After the Pure Blood Statutes, it primarily was a term for Moors and Jews.

Perhaps we have been race-thinking or at least reflecting on what makes human beings different since the beginning of our primary experiences of the world outside ourselves. Since racial thinking is a category of reflecting on otherness and difference, it makes sense to support the idea that thinking about race has been our practice as human beings for a long time. German philosopher and sociologist Jurgen Habermas's concern with 'a philosophy of consciousness' points to the real possibility of race thinking as contingent on the cognitive package carried in the movement from subjectivity to intrasubjective relations.[53]

Awareness of the phenomena of otherness and difference within the human condition suggests that an emergence of a concept of race within the cognitive/reflective and ontic (lived experiences) arena is a frequent, if not necessary, event. Two events seem to take place in this moment of reflection and immanent being: the act of Self-identity (that is Self reflecting on Self) and the classification of "the other." One of the ways we *are appeared to*, as perceptual beings, is in multiple forms of color. Our apprehension of otherness, within the human kaleidoscope, is connected by our sensory apparatus to the color of the person/object (as well as hair texture, eye shape, hue, etc.) and serves as the ground for deciding difference for the perceiver. Once we apprehend another, the culturally influenced, reflective, cognitive processes within us conceptualize 'other people' in terms of racial categories. If Ms. X is of a particular color, has almond shaped eyes, and black straight hair, then Ms. X is (according to our cognitive processes) Asian. Of course, such an assertion about apprehension and reflective determination entails certain philosophical assumptions.

The first philosophical assumption is that there exists an external world that is full of external objects that can be apprehended. These objects are knowable and are known to us. Entailed in the assumption is that one of the kinds of external objects is human. Such objects (humans) are conscious, reflective, perceptual, can be rational or irrational, passionate, have the capacity to make moral judgments, and as such, are able to interact with other human objects.

Secondly, these same person/objects do apprehend other same external person/objects. Here we are reminded of the processes of intra-subjective relations. If these object/persons do not have the ability to apprehend each other, then communication, social construction, moral training, etc. would be impossible. The fact that we do engage, communicate with, and strive for communal intra-personal connections affirms the philosophical assumption that person/objects of the external world do apprehend one another and move to a knowing kind of relationship. That intra-personal phenomenon gives way to concretizing otherness and difference: the given-ness of the "other" and the quality of "how different" is real. Thus, the matrix of human otherness and difference is not the product of imaginations. It is a principal way in which human beings organize and make sense of the world in which we live.

The third assumption rests upon the claim that in our apprehension of other person/objects, we find their characteristics, qualities, and traits are distinguishable, and, in reflection and as such, we conclude that the distinguishable qualities perceived are either a) essential to object, or b) accidental to the person/object. We ask ourselves, "Would Ms. X still be Ms. X if Ms. X was male instead of female or black instead of white?"[54] The fact is that we are constantly evaluating the distinguishable characteristics of other persons. By doing so, we are trying to gain knowledge of the other as to how such characteristics, qualities, and traits affect or do not affect the nature of the other person. This chapter presents one of the ways in which we try to resolve the issue of otherness and difference within the context of race.

In the Introduction, I posited that there exist four main and operative ways in which we, who live the West, think and conceive of race. These four racial concepts have been bequeathed to us by our European-American history and continue to be operative on the sophisticated epistemological level as well as within the realm of common folk psychology/philosophy. It was within the socio-political context of European expansion, colonialization, and imperialism that the phenomenon of human awareness of difference and otherness was concretely transformed into conceptual, paradigmatic concepts of race.[55] This chapter will concentrate on racial essentialism, otherwise known as biological race. Racial essentialism has been the most dominant concept of race in the contemporary arena. While many academics dismiss this concept as faulted and unworthy of consideration, the emergence of white nationalism and the alt-right proves that many people in the United States still adhere to this concept of race.

In this chapter, I will do three things. First, I will discuss the fundamental structure and tenets of racial essentialism. Second, I will present two forms of this concept: racial naturalism (my term) and race as a genetic result. Finally, I will show why racial essentialism, in either form or any form, fails as a coherent concept of race.

The Structure of Racial Essentialism

Racial essentialism originated from a philosophical position known as essentialism. Essentialism, by definition, "is the claim that for every specific kind of entity, it is at least theoretically possible to specify a finite list of characteristics, all of which must have to belong to the group defined."[56] Essentialism tries to posit the nature of things by discovery of the fundamental traits, qualities, and/or characteristics of the thing. Plato argued that things in the phenomenal were representative of the thing in the noumenal. Given his dualistic idea of reality, the essence of the thing is found in the noumenal, while the essence of humans is the soul trapped in a physical body. The discovery of the essential nature of humans was a pedagogical midwifery which allowed the person to come to a self-awareness of truth. Ignorance, for Plato, was the enemy to finding one's essence.[57]

Aristotle, in opposition to Plato's account, suggested that all things were comprised of two basic sides: form and matter (or substance). It was form that gave matter its "quiddity" or "whatness." Form decided the true nature of the thing. Of course, form was open to discovery. The essence of the thing, for Aristotle, was a necessary part of the thing itself, and as such, had certain characteristics open to observation.

The necessary and perceptible character of quiddity allows the observer to rightly classify the thing, separating it from other things in the world. The Aristotelian idea of essence was later employed by St. Thomas Aquinas in the medieval period. Philosopher Naomi Zack states,

> According to Aristotelian and Thomistic doctrines of essence and substance, things are what they are because they contain the essences of the kinds to which they belong: essences (somehow) inhere in individual things that are substances; and the essences of substances support their accidental attributes. Words that refer to kinds of things have definitions that describe the essences of those kinds.[58]

The Aristotelian theory of essence was imported into a critical concept of race and in doing so created the concept known as racial essentialism.

The Tenets of Racial Essentialism

Racial essentialism rests on three main tenets. The **first** main tenet is that there exist three or four main human subgroups.[59] Most racial essentialists label these subgroups as Black (African-American), White (referred to as Anglo-American), Asian, and Hispanic (or Latino). Other racialized subgroups exist but these four dominate our racial discussion. They are called races. Each subgroup owns necessary traits which all individuals of the subgroup share in common, thus, making it possible for individuals to be categorized.

The **second** racial essentialist tenet upholds a belief in a biological foundationalism. Biological foundationalism, in the ordinary sense, is *a body of knowledge that asserts that all facts, ideas, and states of affairs concerning human beings can be either affirmed or denied by biological-genetic evidence.* In the case of racial essentialism, biological foundationalism means that *there is a scientific (biological/genetic) foundation for racial classification.* Racial essentialism supports that the designation of the human species into human subgroups or races can be biologically/genetically verified. Thus, the designation of the human species into subgroups (races) is not an act of prejudice or of social construction.

> Although different races have different histories and cultures, their histories and cultures are not part of the biological foundation of racial differences. This biological foundation has value-neutral or factual support from science and if a racial term is attributed to an individual, then something factual has been said about her.[60]

It is rather a justified categorizing of the human species by the essential characteristics of each subgroup, verified by science. Therefore, the designation of the races, according to this concept of race, is grounded in biological science's ability to establish conclusively the particular traits of each subgroup that are universally part of each member of the subgroup. Since the characteristics, qualities, and traits of each subgroup are perceptible, bio-genetic science's ability to verify their existence is unquestionable.

The **third** racial essential tenet is the belief that the essential characteristics of each subgroup and its members determine the physical, intellectual, and moral disposition of the subgroup and its members. If essential properties determine the nature of the thing, and an individual's physical, intellectual, and moral capacities are part of one's nature, then the essential qualities determine an individual's physical, mental, and moral capacity.

Given the above tenets, racial essentialism may be structured in the following form:

1. The perceptible characteristics, qualities, and/or traits of a subgroup (race) constitute the essence of the subgroup (race).
2. Every individual member of a subgroup (race) possesses (as an individual essence) the perceptible characteristics, qualities, and/ or traits (essence) of the subgroup. The essential characteristics of each subgroup and its members are biologically verifiable.
3. The essential characteristics, qualities, and/or traits of the subgroup and its members are determinant of the physical, intellectual, and/or moral ability of the subgroup and its members.

Racial essentialist conclude definitively that race *is the natural and therefore necessary division of humanity into subgroups according to their essential nature(s).* This division of humanity shown by the differences in essences, preliminarily indicated by morphology, is verifiable by biology. The difference is not accidental but is the necessary result of either a Creator's divine purpose (the essentialist theological position) or by natural/evolutionary processes. We may also conclude that each racial group, by the division, has certain heritable characteristics, traits, and/or qualities that: a) distinguishes the racial group in question from other racial groups; and b) contributes fundamentally to the nature of everyone within the group. Subsequently, the heritable characteristics, traits, and/or qualities affect and decide the intellectual, physiological and moral ability of each member of the group, as well as the overall ability of the group itself. Therefore, by definition,

> S is of a member racial group R if and only if S has the heritable characteristics, traits, and/or qualities unique to group R; and those heritable characteristics are essential

to S such that the heritable characteristics, traits, and/
or qualities determine the intellectual, physical and/ or
moral capacity of S.

Race, given the racial essentialist position, has an epistemological,
ontological, and ethical status. Epistemologically, racial essentialism
asserts that the race of a person is conclusively demonstrable and
the validity of the claim of racial demonstrability is warranted by a
scientific/biological foundation.[61] Given the scientific under girding,
the race of any person can be known and therefore gives a teleological
type of knowledge to the knower. The teleological knowledge allows
the knower to justifiably classify humanity into distinct types (races).
Given the demonstrability of race, the subject can package a justifiable
"racial knowledge."[62] The scientific character of the racial knowledge
bolsters the classifying activity as rationally grounded; thus, any belief
generated about race is properly part of the subject's noetic structure
causing no event of cognitive dysfunction. The subject has epistemic
justification in making racial claims about the object of thought.

Race, under the racial essentialist umbrella, has ontological
status in that it asserts that the race of an individual qualitatively
figures out the fundamental being (essence) of the individual qua
individual. The essentialist's position claims unequivocally that race
is the determinant factor of the physical, intellectual, and moral
ability of a person (if S is a member of R, then S can do x and y,
but not z). The scientific foundation allows one to accentuate the
ontological "difference" of the races. Taylor writes,

> On the theoretical level this meant dividing humanity into
> deeply distinct but still related varieties. [Races were seen]
> as essentially distinct types. This distinctness was taken
> to be the result of processes that were not external but
> internal, involving the heritability of essential traits across
> generations. Adherents to this new reading of race as type
> assumed that the deep differences between humans were
> intimately related to measurable differences in human
> bodies.[63]

The differences, say the racial essentialists, have monumental
significance. While every individual is human, *how one is a human,*

individually, is radically decided by her racial designation. Issues of volition, moral agency, intellectual ability, etc. are all decided by race and are asserted to be scientifically verifiable.

The German philosopher G.W.F. Hegel, who was convinced that such an essentialist position was undeniable, stated about Africans and Asians that,

> They [African descendants] do not attain to the feeling of human personality, their mentality is quite dormant, and remaining sunk in itself and making no progress, and thus corresponding to the compact, differenceless mass of the African continent ... The Mongols [Asians], on the other hand, rise above this childish naiveté; they reveal as their characteristic feature a restless mobility which comes to no fixed result ....[64]

The ethical component of the racial essentialism position is quite interesting. Knowledge of race empowers the person in her epistemic obligation to self and others. Because the racial essence influences the ranking of races, the more she knows about her racial designation, the more she knows of her moral potential. The higher the race in the hierarchy, the more morally capable the individual is.

> ... by the latter half of the nineteenth century, ... American scientists constructed speculative theories of the hierarchy of human races, based on philosophical essentialism. These scientists posited a unique essence or "genius" for each race that was present in all its members: in cultural and biological rank, the white race was highest, the black race lowest; the essence of the black race was infinitely transmittable from one generation of direct genealogical descent to the next, but the essence of the white race could only be preserved if the essence of the black race were not present with it in the same individual.[65]

Knowing where she is on the race hierarchy informs her moral obligation as an agent. If she is high on the rank and pure in race, she has a higher moral vision, capacity, and obligation, than those who are lower in racial status. If she is of one of the lower racial levels, then her moral obligation is greatly diminished. For the racial essentialist, race affects one's moral agency in every respect.

Philosopher Kwame Anthony Appiah insists that adoption of racial essentialism creates two very interesting moral attitudes regarding other races.[66] Given the racial essentialism model, one becomes either an extrinsic racist or an intrinsic racist.[67] By racist, Appiah means one that participates in and adheres to a body of knowledge concerning the nature of race. An extrinsic racist is one who, "makes moral distinction between members of different races because they believe that the racial essence entails certain morally relevant qualities."[68]

> The basis for the extrinsic racists' discrimination between people is their belief that members of different races differ in respects that *warrant* the differential treatment – respects, like honesty or courage or intelligence, that are uncontroversially held (at least by most contemporary cultures) to be acceptable as a basis for treating people differently.[69]

Appiah believes that the extrinsic racists can change his moral attitude given proper information about race (in Appiah's case, the proper information would be that "race" does not exist). The problem of the extrinsic racist is epistemic.

Intrinsic racists "are people who differentiate morally between members of different races because they believe that each race has a different moral status quite independent of the moral characteristics entailed by its racial essence."[70]

> Just as, for example, many people assume that the bare fact that they are biologically related to another person … gives them a moral interest in that person, so an intrinsic racist holds that the bare fact of being of the same race is a reason for preferring one person to another. For an intrinsic racist, no amount of evidence that a member of another race is capable of great moral, intellectual, or cultural achievements, or has characteristics that, in members of one's own race, would make them admirable or attractive, offers any ground for treating that person as she would treat similarly endowed members of her own race.[71]

This attribute of intrinsic racists cannot be swayed by rational discourse. It is as if they suffer from cognitive dysfunction. They are beyond the pale of reason.

As one can see, the racial essentialist position creates an environment where knowledge of the ethical potential of other races also informs S of the moral potential of other races. If all races have heritable characteristics, traits, and/or qualities, then knowledge of those characteristics gives valuable and credible insight into the nature of every member of the racial group S may encounter. S may expect more or less of racialized others depending on where they rank on the racial scale. Therefore, according to the racial essentialist position, race has epistemic, ontological, and ethical importance. Now we shall examine two forms of racial essentialism: racial naturalism and DuBoisian essentialism.

The Case for Racial (essentialist) Naturalism

The nineteenth century marked the emergence of racial essentialism as the dominant concept of race in Western culture. It offered the best of both worlds: an intellectual idea about race that seemed to have scientific and philosophical validity. It was undoubtedly persuasive and uncompromisingly seductive. By experiential, scientific, anthropological, and historical observation, certain 'facts' made racial essentialism unquestionable. It was clear that a) there were different races; b) the different races demonstrated a hierarchical structure evidenced by European cultural superiority when compared to other newly "discovered" cultures; and c) these "other" people were demonstrably intellectually and morally inferior. Based on the reports of expeditions to the "New World" and Africa, European culture was clearly, to these observers, the superior culture among cultures. Science had proven it and philosophy had demonstrated it: racial classification was in full gear by the end of the nineteenth century.

The beginning of the twentieth century carries the same racial essentialist assumptions of the nineteenth with, however, additional social scientific support. The Social Darwinists, influenced by Darwin's evolutionary theory, attempted to combine essentialism with social scientific observation.[72] United with Social Darwinism, racial essentialism took a new twist. It was now sociologically demonstrable that certain races were evolutionarily marked to be at the top or bottom of the social hierarchy.[73]

What emerged in the midst of this social development was a new version of racial essentialism that I call "racial naturalism." The argument for racial (essentialist) naturalism suggests the following.

1. Given the presence of human subgroups, race is a natural phenomenon.

The natural world is a constitutive whole of real things and occurrences. These real things would be like waterfalls, rocks, birds, etc. One of the other real occurrences in the natural world is the occurrence of race. Race is the product of natural evolutionary processes and as such is as natural as flowers, bees and other things of nature.

2. All real entities and occurrences of the natural world are scientifically demonstrable, measurable, and/or observable.

This assumption has been affirmed since Descartes. The underlying presupposition of the Cartesian external world (*res extensa*) is that the external world and its properties (i.e. rocks, trees, etc.) are measurable, demonstrable, and observable. The ability of external properties to be demonstrated scientifically is proof that those things are real. Racial naturalists insist that race fits this criterion because it can and is provable by biology and the social sciences, and therefore, like all other properties of the external world, must be considered real.

3. All real entities and occurrences of the natural, external world have an essence.

Since Aristotle, one the definitions of "being" has been that all things that "are" consist of a form and substance. Quiddity or the "what-ness" is created by the essence of the thing. Science verifies the presence of a racial essence. Again, race conforms to this criterion.

4. Therefore, given that race fulfills the necessary and sufficient conditions of 1-3, race is a real and natural phenomenon.

I suggest all philosophical positions argue both for and against some other philosophical position(s). The philosophical concept of race that racial naturalism argues against is the idea that race is merely a social construction and therefore is not real.

> [P]aradigm cases of real things – rocks, tree, the sun, wombats – -are what they are, wherever they are, whatever we say about them. But the basic underlying reality is whatever it is, and we're just right or wrong about it.[74]

The basic underlying reality in terms of race, say the racial naturalists, is that race is real like the wombat or the sun. All three – the wombat, the sun, and race – are: a) natural, b) scientifically demonstrable, and c) possessing an essence. The sheer power of argument makes racial naturalism a formidable concept of race. We turn our attention now to DuBoisian essentialism.

DuBoisian Essentialism

William Edward Burghart Du Bois (1868-1963) formulated one of the most powerful and intriguing forms of racial essentialism. Du Bois was an African-American author, philosopher, social constructionist, and Pan-Africanist. He was greatly influenced by the philosophical systems of Kant, Herder, and Hegel. His social scientific analysis demonstrated that he was a product of the German Historical School of Economics in general and an intellectual disciple of Gustav Schmoller in particular.[75] Our focus here is on the Du Bois form of racial essentialism.

Du Bois is troubled by racial essentialism's claim that science has proven the inferiority of Africans and African Americans. While not directly mentioned, I take it his objection would be against scientific inferiority of all races except Caucasian. He posits that, "what matters are not the grosser physical differences" but the "differences subtle, delicate and elusive, though they may be – which have silently but definitely separated men into groups."[76] Observe his statement from "The Conservation of Races."

> While these subtle forces have generally followed the natural cleavage of common blood, descent and physical peculiarities, they have at other times swept across and ignored these. At all times, however, they have divided human beings into races, which, while they perhaps transcend scientific definition, nevertheless, are clearly defined to the eye of the Historian, [Philosopher], and Sociologist.
> ... What, then, is a race? It is a vast family of human beings, generally of common blood and language, always of common history, traditions and impulses, who are both voluntarily and involuntarily striving together for the accomplishment of certain more or less vividly conceived ideals of life.[77]

Clearly, Du Bois is attempting to move away from a biological definition of race, while simultaneously maintaining an essentialist concept of race. What then the essence of race? It is a socio-historical essence that constitutes race for Du Bois.[78] Du Bois asserts that there are eight "distinctly differentiated races." For Du Bois they are: Slavs, Teutons, English (i.e. all Anglos including Anglo Americans), Negroes (i.e. people of African descent), the Romance race, Semites, Hindus, and Mongolians.

Du Bois further enunciates his position.

> The question now is: What is the real distinction between the nations? Is it the physical differences of blood, color and cranial measurements? Certainly we must all acknowledge that physical differences play a great part .... But while race differences have followed mainly physical race lines, yet no mere physical distinctions would really define or explain the deeper differences – the cohesiveness and continuity of these groups. The deeper differences are spiritual, psychical, differences – undoubtedly based on the physical, but infinitely transcending them.[79]

Thus, racial essence for Du Bois is "spiritual – [and] psychical." It is present in each of the races. This spiritual, psychic, racial essence supervenes on the physical, and yet transcends the physical. Racial essence for Du Bois has a teleological purpose as well.

> [Every race is] striving, each in its own way, to develope for civilization its particular message, its particular ideal, which shall help to guide the world nearer and nearer that perfection of human life for which we all long....[80]

The teleological function of a race's racial essence is to enable the race to "develop for civilization its particular message." Du Bois believes that the African American race has yet to develop its message. However, the first stages of the "Negro message" has emerged. The first stages of develop of the Negro message is cast in religious worship and music.[81]

We can summarize Du Bois' essentialism in the following way.

1. There exists a racial essence.
2. That racial essence is not scientific but is socio-historical. It supervenes upon the physical but transcends it.
3. The socio-historical essence of a race has a teleological function. Racial essence enables the race to develop a particular message for civilization (i.e. humanity as a whole).

While racial essentialism in both forms is seductive, I suggest that the internal problems with this concept of race force us in the end to reject them. I now present the problems that defeat racial essentialism.

Arguments against Racial Essentialism

While in many ways racial essentialism presents itself as a competent concept of race, three main problems surface when the concept is analyzed closely: a biological problem, an ethical (moral) problem, and an ontological (metaphysical) problem.

For the sake of clarity, I will re-state the argument for racial essentialism. It claims:

1. Humanity can be divided into X number of distinct subgroups (races). This division can be accomplished exhaustively such that no person would be a member of more than one subgroup (race).
2. Each subgroup possesses a unique set of "heritable," and perceptible characteristics, qualities, and/or traits. These unique characteristics, qualities, and/or traits constitute the essence of the subgroup (race).
3. Every individual member of a subgroup possesses the unique perceptible characteristics, qualities, and/or traits (the essence) of the subgroup.
4. The essential characteristics of each subgroup and its members are biologically verifiable.
5. The essential characteristics, qualities, and/or traits of the subgroup and its members are determinant of the physical, intellectual, and/or moral ability of the subgroup and its members.

Given the above argument, it seems to me that racial essentialism claims that races are distinct, mutually exclusive types or subgroups. They also claim this alleged 'fact' is verified by biology, but, upon further examination, we find that the argument is counter-factual. **Problem one**: there is no biological evidence that races are distinct, mutually exclusive subgroups. In fact, the biological/genetic evidence seems to be just the opposite: subgroups may differ in morphology, but genetically they are connected and interrelated.[82] Appiah writes,

> The classification of peoples into "races" would be biologically interesting if both the margins and the migrations had not left behind a genetic trail. But they have, and along the trail are millions of us (humans) who can be fitted into no plausible scheme at all.[83]

It is clear that over the centuries of human interaction, there no longer exist any pure races (if any ever existed in the first place). If there is no such thing as racial purity, then there can be no racial essence which biology could verify. There are physical, morphological differences, but not of kind, simply of degree.

Racial essentialism might counter that there does exist a racial essence, but it is larger than the scope of our scientific technology. The racial essence is "spiritual" or "psychical" (i.e. DuBoisian). But, the promise of racial essentialism is that the quiddity of race can be biologically verified. Clearly that claim is false.

> ... science sought in a heritable racial essence an explanation of what its proponents took to be the observed phenomena of the differential distribution in human populations both of morphological and of psychological and social traits. What modern genetics shows is that there is no such underlying racial essence.[84]

This quote from Appiah brings us to my **second problem** with racial essentialism. It claims that races have heritable characteristics that determine intellectual, social, and moral qualities. According to that position, the intellectual, social, and moral character of a person is determined by one's racial essence. Racial essentialists built from this a hierarchy of the races, such that any member of the white race would be of more excellent moral character, more intellectually gifted, more socially appropriate, etc., than any other member of a different race. In keeping with the argument, a member of the black race (because black was at the bottom of the hierarchy) would be of marginal intellect, suspect moral character, etc. If the racial essentialist claim is correct, no person of another race can be as moral as a member of the white race.

Observe the following thought process.

> Jim is white and Joe is black. Jim and Joe are walking together to the store. Joe sees a twenty-dollar bill on the ground and suggests to his partner Jim, "Let's take this $20.00 to the store clerk and see if anyone has lost it." Upon arriving at the front door, an elderly white lady is shuffling through her bag. The boys ask, "What's wrong, lady?"
>
> "I've lost my money, a twenty-dollar bill, and I can't buy what I wanted in the store!"
>
> "Lady," said Jim, "we found $20.00 on the side walk."
>
> "And we want you to have it," Joe exclaimed.
>
> The boys gave the woman the twenty dollars, happy that they had found the money, and given it to the elderly lady.

First, is it possible that two people of different races could agree to do something that is morally applaudable, and then do as they intended? The answer must be, Yes. History demonstrates that in times of mutual respect, need, love, and/or tragedy, human beings of different racial groups have joined together for a common good. If racial essentialism is correct it would be impossible for Joe to have acted with moral integrity because of his racial essence. But the story is not counter-intuitive, nor counter-factual of similar historical events.

Something about being human says that every rational person is responsible for their moral agency, and that race cannot be a cause for exemption. If racial essentialism is correct, members of a particular race are guaranteed to be the most intellectually and morally gifted, while members of another race are doomed to failure.

> The disappearance of a widespread belief in the biological category of the Negro would leave nothing for the (negative) racist to have an attitude toward. Let me put the claim at its weakest: in the absence of a racial essence, there could be no guarantee that some particular person was not more gifted – in some respect – than any or all others in the populations of other regions (other races).[85]

Clearly, our common cultural history, our personal experiences, and our individual intuition tell that racial essentialism is in error.

Is it possible that racial essentialism is true ontologically, while false biologically and ethically? Racial essentialism maintains that there exist racial qualities, both perceptible and heritable, shared by all people in their subgroup. Is it possible we have the biology wrong and have not rightly connected these qualities (essence) to moral and intellectual capacities? No, because these qualities supervene on the physical. They are spiritual (metaphysical) and thus fall outside scientific verification.

The third problem, the problem of ontology, arises with this thought: If the racial essence of an individual is spiritual, does not such a position commit us to a dualistic ontology? If the essence is spiritual, then to what does this essence adhere? If essence adheres to our spiritual constitution, what part is our spiritual constitution contained in and how may we measure, examine, and/or evaluate it? Do we need spiritual instruments? What are they? And finally, does not such a metaphysical concept force us ultimately to view ourselves as "ghosts in a machine?"[86]

If the spiritual, racial essence adheres to our physicality, how does it do so? Can two different substances intermingle? If so, how is this process accomplished? It seems that the DuBoisian model does not help. Du Bois does not tell us how we acquire a spiritual racial essence. Biology has shown us that a biological racial essence does not exist. So, because of a lack of evidence, we must also reject racial essentialism on metaphysical grounds.

Because racial essentialism fails the biological, moral, and metaphysical tests, we must conclude that racial essentialism is false. The argument against racial essentialism states:

1. Racial essentialism claims humans can be divided into mutually distinct subgroups by their distinctive, racial characteristics (racial essence); however, since there is no biological evidence that subgroups are mutually distinct, there can be no distinctive racial characteristics and, hence, no racial essence.

2. Racial essentialism claims that racial characteristics (racial essence) determine a race's intellectual and moral ability; however, without distinctive racial characteristics (racial essence) (See #1), their claim is false.

3. Racial essentialism states that racial essence is physical (and thus biologically and genetically verifiable) or spiritual (metaphysical) and outside the scope of science. Since there is no biological evidence to show subgroups are mutually distinct and we have no instruments to measure the metaphysical, the theory of a "racial essence" is false.

Some would argue that a concept of race as a whole is false. The proponents of this idea conclude that race is merely a social construction and thus ultimately, objectively non-existent.

> Race-talk is a way of denoting the populations that we've been discussing all along. This enables us to say that a person we'd

call Black – is more likely to live in substandard or overcrowded housing, or lack health insurance, or be unemployed, than someone we'd call white. [I]t also enables us to say that this same person is more likely to be, or to have been, in the criminal system or to perform less well in school.

[But] being Black is no longer an explanation for anything. It becomes, instead, a gesture at a request for an explanation –. All of this is to say: our Western races are social constructs.[87]

This idea about race may be correct, but it is premature to adopt it now. In the next chapter we will examine a concept of race as a social construct, but real. Therefore, we suspend our judgment about race as a concept for a while.

Chapter 3

RACE AS A SOCIAL CONSTRUCT
WITH OBJECTIVE STATUS

In Chapter 2, we saw the advance and later failure of racial essentialism as a viable concept of race. Its failure is and was due to three main problems. First, it was shown that racial essentialism relies on a faulty biological foundation that claimed: a) the ability to prove a racial essence that was unique for each racial subgroup; and, b) the ability to name heritable racial characteristics, traits, and/or qualities that decide the intellectual and moral ability of races. The foundation is faulty because modern science indicates that such a claim is false in both regards. Research in biology and genetics suggests that there is no evidence of unique heritable characteristics particular to races, and subsequently, there is no evidence for the existence of a racial essence. Racial essentialism is counterfactual and fails as an adequate concept of race.

Secondly, racial essentialism fails because it advocates an ethical determinism with its theory of a racial essence, which essence denies individual free-will and personal responsibility. Commitment to the belief in racial essence entails an abandonment of the belief in human autonomy. If one's intellectual and moral capacity is determined by one's racial essence, then the person cannot be responsible for her individual actions since all actions are pre-determined by one's inherited racial characteristics, traits, and/or qualities. One simply acts in accordance to one's nature. The adherence to such a moral claim is at least counter-intuitive, historically false, and ultimately dangerous. Therefore, on intuitive, historical, and ethical grounds, racial essentialism was rejected.

Finally, racial essentialism advances a problematic metaphysical claim regarding the constitution of human beings that, in the end, is incongruous. If we align with naturalistic racial essentialism, we must say that individual human beings have a racial essence distinct and separate from the physical body committing us to a dualistic ontology. This drenches us in all the classical Rylian problems of dualism. English philosopher Gilbert Ryle challenged Cartesian dualism by suggesting if we take dualism seriously, the result makes us "ghosts in a machine." Given Ryle's analysis combined with the racial essentialist theory, we become "colored ghosts in machines."[88]

By aligning with DuBoisian essentialism, we must commit to an idea that racial essences somehow supervene on the physical by some spiritual or psychical process. This idea stirs up a two-part question: How does such a connection occur and what is the evidence of such an interaction? Unfortunately, this question is never answered by the DuBoisian essentialists. At the end of our analysis of racial essentialism, we must conclude that the position is false and we are left with the previous question of this project, "What is race?"

Sally Haslanger states the problem in answering the question of race in the following manner.

> The self-evidence of racial distinctions in everyday American life is at striking odds with the uncertainty about the category of race in law and the academy. Work in the biological sciences has informed us that our practices of racial categorization don't map neatly onto any useful biological classification; but that doesn't settle much, if anything. For what should we make of our tendency to classify individuals according to race, apparently on the basis of physical appearance? And what are we to make of the social and economic consequences of such classifications? Is race real or is it not?[89]

Since racial essentialism provided us with an unsatisfactory answer to the question of race, another concept of race is needed for our analysis of the phenomenon of difference and otherness within the context of race. The new concept will demand a paradigmatic shift in thinking about race. Seeing as we cannot find a scientific justification for thinking about race in an essentialist manner, a new paradigm must emerge if we are to think and speak lucidly about race. The new paradigm is social constructionism.

I. Race as a Social Construct

The concept of race as a social construct has become the most popular categorization of race, in the intellectual community, for the last few years.[90] It is a position advanced throughout various disciplines of the academy. In this chapter, we will investigate the argument that even though race is a social construct, race has an objective status. The social construct conclusion will be that since race has an objective status, race is real.

A. Social Constructionism

What is a social construction (or, social construct) and what is meant by *race is a social construct*? Most advocates of the school of social constructionism define a social construct as an idea, which may appear to be natural and obvious to those who accept it, but in actuality, is an invention or artifact of a particular culture or society.[91] What is entailed in this idea is that social constructs are a matter of human creation and ingenuity, not constructions of God or natural kinds like rocks, suns or electrons. Included in the list of social constructs are all institutions, language, money, and religion. Some would argue that our complete conceptual framework – including ethics, metaphysics, and epistemology – is a social construct.[92]

Social constructs are of two forms: weak and strong.[93] Weak social constructs are "...categories...[that] exist only because people tacitly agree to act as if they exist. Examples include money, tenure, citizenship, decorations for bravery, and the presidency of the United States."[94] Weak social constructs demand repeated human practice and take on the sense of universal acceptability after frequent and repetitive interaction. For example, in Anglo American culture, hand-shaking is commonly agreed upon as a proper greeting and sign of friendship as opposed to kissing on both cheeks as in France. Both actions are greeting gestures created by human beings and supported by culture. They supply the *sufficient* conditions but not the *necessary* ones for weak social constructs. In this society, we have tacitly agreed that hand-shaking is the primary form of greeting, but not necessarily a sign of friendship (it could mean I have no weapon). Hand-shaking does not exclude kissing as a right act of greeting, it simply has been preferred within this socio-cultural context. Handshaking merely provides the *sufficient* conditions for friendship, but not the *necessary* conditions. Anglo American society tacitly agrees that hand-shaking is the proper social expression for greeting and showing friendship. Once the agreement and universal acceptability of a society is in place, the sign (hand-shaking) is transformed into a social convention which in turn becomes a social construct.

Strong social constructs are categories that are openly stated and agreed upon by the majority of a particular historical and social community. They are supported by convention and public opinion and are grounded in socio-political institutions. Strong social constructs then are:

> ... a highly elaborated set of conventions brought forth by one particular culture (our own) in the circumstances of one particular historical period; thus, it is not, as the standard view would have it, a body of knowledge and testable conjecture concerning the real world. It is a discourse, devised by and for one specialized interpretive community, under terms created by the complex net of social circumstance, political opinion, economic incentive and ideological climate that constitutes the ineluctable human environment ... Consequently, its truth claims are irreducibly self-referential, in that they can be upheld only by appeal to the standards that define the ... community and distinguish it from other social formations.[95]

Social constructs – in the strong sense – are elaborate and discursive in nature. They are the innovation of Western culture verified by our continuous participation and or use of them as definitive of everyday reality.[96]

According to this position, race(s) would be classified as *strong social constructs*. The social construct argument would posit that over the centuries, starting in Europe, race has been constructed by European and further elaborated by Anglo American culture. The same culture has provided individuals within society with an "elaborate set of conventions" for how to think about its constructs, including race. To be sure, non-Anglo European societies – as well as Asian and Latino societies – have ideas about race. But the most dominant form of racial classification that affects the contemporary American landscape comes from a Western European ideology. How we think about race is traceable to the racial anthropologic and philosophical ideas of Western Europe.

Because race is a strong social construct, there is also "a discourse" about race which continues to become more elaborate and complex as the social circumstance, political opinion, economic welfare, and ideological climate increases in complexity and influence upon the concept of race. The preliminary argument for race as a social construct, in the strong sense, is as follows:

1. In our current society, strong social constructs exist and are taken for granted by members of this culture.
2. Race is a strong social construct.
3. Strong social constructs possess the quality of appearing inevitable.
4. Social constructs need not to have existed; or, need not exist in their present form.
5. Nature or God does not determine social constructs.
6. Thus, social constructs are not inevitable.

A question arises given the above argument. If social constructs are not inevitable, and race is a social construct, are social constructs, including race, real?

Ian Hacking suggests that, "...there need not always be a conflict between saying that [X is] 'socially constructed' and saying that [it is] real."[97] The above argument may be positing a comment on our conceptualizing of things. It may be that our ideas about things are not inevitable and not that the object of our thought is not inevitable. More will be said about this way of interpreting the argument from social constructionism as we narrow our focus on racial social constructionism. But this reading of what is being said in the above argument needs to be held. What is clear is that premise 6 opens the door to two possible conclusions:

7. Social constructs, including race, are not real; or,

7*. Social constructs, including race, are real in some other way.

At this point we focus on what, from now on in this chapter, is called racial social constructionism and which conclusion we come to.

B. Racial Social Constructionism: Traditional and Radical

Paul Taylor suggests that though racial essentialism (which he called "classical racialism") has failed to provide a satisfactory concept of race, we must continue to explore the phenomenon of difference and otherness within the context of race.

> People still use the language of race and they thereby impose on us the burden of understanding how they use it and what they use it to do. But even if that's right, it doesn't tell us anything about the ontological commitments that come with this language. That is, it doesn't yet answer these questions: What does Western race-talk point to, what realities does it denote, if not the impossible populations of classical racialism? [98]

Taylor goes on to propose that two ontological choices lie before us regarding the reality of race: skepticism and realism.[99] Skepticism would result in stating that there is no referent to which racial language points, thus race does not exist. Realism would suggest that there is a referent for racial language and that race is real in some sense other than racial essentialism. Charles Mills offers an intriguing perspective for our analysis.[100]

Mills suggests that in analyzing our options regarding the categorizing of concepts of race, we should borrow from metaphysics and science.[101]

> Terminology developed elsewhere can illuminatingly be drawn upon to map representative positions on the ontology of race. As we know, philosophers of science and ethicists have an elaborate vocabulary for demarcating contrasting views on the reality of scientific entities and the metaphysics of moral value – realism, constructivism, conventional/relativism, instrumentalism, subjectivism, non-cognitivism, nihilism/error theories, and so forth. Some of this vocabulary can usefully be appropriated to clarify debates on race. The correspondences are not exact and should not be pressed too far; moreover, some terms have no plausible "racial" equivalent ... Still, I expect the similarity that emerges to be ... enlightening.[102]

Mills suggests two umbrella categories for the "metaphysics of race."[103] The first he calls "objectivism." The second umbrella category he labels as "anti-objectivism." At this point, let us focus on the objectivist arguments for race as a social construct. Later in this project we will consider the anti-objectivist nihilistic argument regarding race as a social construct.

Mills states, as a definition for objectivism, that: "it connotes the independence of what we choose, what we believe."[104] Under the objectivist category he places as subcategories realism and constructivism.[105] What is a racial realist?

> A "racial realist" in the most minimal sense will be somebody who thinks it is objectively the case – independent of human belief – that there are natural human races; in other words, that races are natural kinds.[106]

Taylor refers to racial realists as classical racialists and I have termed such thinkers as racial essentialists. Mills' sub-category of constructionists needs to be expanded to include radical constructionist (to which Taylor labels himself) as opposed to traditional constructionists like Mills.

Traditional racial constructivism, "… involves an actual agreement of some under conditions where the constraints are not epistemic … but *political* …; the "idealization" is pragmatic… [A]n objective ontological status is involved which arises out of *intersubjectivity*, and which… is real…."[107] Race has, for the traditional racial constructionist, an objective ontological status because it is part of a social reality. Mills states:

> I am not claiming that race is the only principle of social hierarchy, or that racial struggle is the comprehensive key to understanding history, or that individuals' racial ontology is in all circumstances the most important thing about them. But systematic racial privilege has been an undeniable (though often denied) fact in recent global history, and exploring an ontology of race will contribute to … our understanding of social dynamics…. One's racial category has been taken as saying a great deal about what and who one is, more fundamentally.[108]

So, the traditional racial constructionist argument may be presented in the following manner.

8. (Assuming 7*) Some social constructs have an objective ontological status that arises out of the intersubjectivity of a common and particular cultural-social reality.
9. Race is a social construct that has an objective ontological status by virtue of the intersubjectivity that arises out of experienced reality.
10. Therefore, race as a social construct is real.

Radical racial constructionists agree with traditionalists that race is a social construct but disagree as to what constitutes the objective status of race. Paul C. Taylor, a radical racial constructionist, asserts that:

> … our Western races are social constructs. They are things that we humans create in the transactions that define social life. Specifically, they are the probabilistically defined populations that result from the white supremacist determination to link appearance and ancestry to social location and life chances. [109]

Taylor defines "race-thinking as a way of assigning meaning to human bodies and bloodlines" and, because race depends on "the existence of human agreements" for its existence, race cannot have objective ontological status.[110] However, race does have an "epistemically objective" status due to human conventions. Taylor states,

> Race-thinking varies from society to society, which shows that it depends on local human conventions for its existence. But once the conventions are established ... then there are facts that exist independently of any individual's particular judgments and beliefs. So there are things, like money [and race], that seem real without being ontologically objective.[111]

In sum, race is *ontologically subjective* but *epistemically objective.*

We see how the two positions differ. The traditional racial constructionist posits for race an objective ontological status that arises out of our common cultural-societal intersubjective reality. The radical racial constructionist maintains that race as a construct is "ontologically subjective, but epistemically objective" due to social conventions. Casting the radical racial constructionist argument is very interesting. Beginning the argument from 7*, it would move in the following manner for the radical racial constructionist (note: to distinguish arguments I will use the * sign for the radical racial constructionist):

8*. Some social constructs have a subjective ontological status but an objective epistemic status.

9*. The objective epistemic status of some social constructs is by human convention(s).

10*. Race is a social construct that has a subjective ontological status but an objective epistemic status by human convention(s).

11*. Therefore, race, as a social construct, is real.

One can easily see that both the traditional racial constructionist and the radical racial constructionist converge on several different points.

- Both agree that race is a social construct that is constantly taken as the given in Western culture.
- Both agree that race is spoken of and appears to be inevitable, but, race is not inevitable.
- Both agree that race need not to have existed (or need not to exist as it does) in contemporary Western culture.
- Both agree that Western European, Anglo American history is of monumental influence on the concept of race.
- Finally, they both agree that race as a social construct has an objective status.

The two racial constructionist positions diverge, however, as to how race is objective and what supports race's objectivity. For the traditional racial constructionist, the intersubjective activity of persons within a particular historical context gives race an ontological objective status. The radical racial constructionist points to human social convention as the ground for race's objective epistemic status. For the traditionalist, race's objective status is metaphysical, grounded in a social ontological reality. The social ontological reality from which race emerges is one that has been shaped and promulgated by our Western European, Anglo-American history.[112]

The radical constructionist agrees that the social context is paramount to a concept of race. The radical constructionist, however, points to the structure of conventions as to the birthing and nurturing context for the objective status of race, and not just the mere inter-play of human beings in a particular culture in a particular historical moment. The radical constructionist insists that conventions determine our thinking patterns – our cognitive frameworks. Race, as a cognitive entity, is also determined by the same cognitive processes. All of our cognitive processes are determined by the social conventions that structure our lived experiences.

II. Argument Against Race as an Objective Social Construct

The Problem of "Passing"

It must be acknowledged that the social constructionist position is seductive. It seems to alleviate the problems found with racial essentialism and provides us with an alternative answer that appears credible. Social constructionism proposes an answer to the question: "What is race?"

Social constructionism claims:

1. Race is a social construct;
2. Race has an objective ontological status (Mills); or
3. Race has an objective epistemological status (Taylor).
4. Since race, as a social construct, has objective status, race is real.

Upon closer examination of this concept of race, I suggest two problems arise in the elocution of race as a social construct. I propose that the traditional constructionism represented by Mills and the radical constructionism championed by Taylor are both victims of two major problems related to the practice of *passing*.[113]

The first of these problems for both forms of race as a social construct with an objective status is the intentional nature of *passing*. I define "passing" as *the conscious act of an individual, who objectively belongs to one racialized group, but willfully endeavors to belong to another racialized group by appearance, actions, and thinking*. One of my aunts was a very fair-skinned African American woman. For many years my aunt lived as a white woman in America. She adopted classic Anglo mannerisms: vocal quality, dress, social action, etc. She lived the life of a "white" woman for so long that she referred to herself as white and rejected her African American history and family. Many African American women and men willfully chose to live in America as Anglo Americans. One may argue that *passing* was a way to gain privilege and power in a racialized society. Perhaps, but what stands as a point of reflection is that *passing* not only requires acting a part, it also demands believing the part.

The second problem the *passing* phenomenon poses for race as a social construct with objective status is that, by definition, *passing* excludes the accidental or deliberate mislabeling of an individual of one race into another which I call "the Pudd'nhead Wilson Syndrome."[114] As you will remember from Mark Twain's classic text *The Tragedy of Puddn'head Wilson*, Puddn'head Wilson was a child born in slavery who was 1/31 Black. He looked like an Anglo child and was switched at birth and grew up in the master's house. The "Puddn'head Wilson Syndrome," for some thinkers, serves as a form of *passing*, in that an individual of a racialized group is mistaken as a member of another group.

Contrary to philosopher Ron Mallon, who counts the "Puddn'head Syndrome" as a form of *passing*, the real or imagined cases of racial mislabeling do not constitute *passing* because *passing* necessitates an act of volition on the part of the person in question. Thus, the "Pudd'nhead Wilson Syndrome" does not constitute *passing* because a) it is enacted upon an individual by another without consensus (observe that the infants that were switched did not choose to be members of another race); and b) a situation imposed upon by another, without the consensus of the participant, constitutes deception and an inauthentic racially categorized experience (they were not aware of the deception).

One may argue that *passing* is an inauthentic racial experience as well, but I suggest that *passing* by an act of volition and living in a mislabeled experience created by another without consensus, demonstrates differences of kind and not degree. The significant and fundamental difference between *passing* and being mislabeled is that within the act of *passing*, the individual willfully chooses to be of another race. In mislabeling, the individual is robbed of choice – her classification imposed upon her. Choice is essential to what constitutes an act of *passing*.

The same is true (i.e. that mislabeling is not *passing*) regarding real cases like Susie Phipps and Gregory Williams. While these cases command our attention, particularly in the arena of philosophy of law, they do not, by definition, constitute *passing*. These cases demonstrate that neither person chose their mislabeling. It was revealed to them later that they were placed in the wrong racial class.[115] One of the central elements of *passing* is human volition. The individual must willfully choose to be a member of a different racial group other than the one assigned to him by the social construct of his community. The second element of *passing* is that the individual who wills to be a member of a different race will choose a racial group that is perceived as more acceptable to the socially constructed racial hierarchy that is in place within the community. The agent of *passing* chooses a racial group that is deemed superior in status to the one to which she objectively belongs.[116] This second element intuitively makes sense and seems to be present in all acts of *passing*.

Given the social constructionist concept of race, the social phenomenon of *passing* ought to be accounted for within the social constructionist's theory. Mallon writes,

> Passing is problematic for constructionists, since it seems to involve a person objectively belonging to one race while being believed to belong to another. Since constructionist accounts of race aim to offer an account of what race is, these accounts ought also to allow us to understand passing. On the other hand, if a constructionist account cannot make sense of passing, then such accounts must be inadequate to understanding the complexity of race.[117]

The social constructionist *passing* constraint would then read:

> On a constructionist theory of race, the act of passing is possible, [permissible], and explicable.[118]

The philosophical issue here is clear. If social racial constructionism is to provide us with a suitable concept of race, it must be able to explicate the phenomenon of *passing*. If it cannot demonstrate how *passing* is possible, the social constructionist position must be rejected.

Walter Benn Michaels argues that constructionists cannot account for the phenomenon of *passing* and therefore, cannot provide us with an adequate concept of race.[119] Michaels states,

> The very idea of passing – whether it takes the form of looking like you belong to a different race or of acting like you belong to a different race – requires an understanding of race as something separate from the way you look and the way you act…. But if to see race as a social construction is inevitably (even if unwillingly and unknowingly) to essentialize it, then race really is either an essence or an illusion.[120]

Michaels insists that a middle ground does not exist for social constructionists. Either the social constructionist must advance a racial ascription to race groups, which in turn amounts to essentialism, or social constructionists must abandon the concept of race as objectively real. Again, Michaels writes, "for the idea of cultural identity to do any work beyond describing the beliefs people actually hold and the things they actually do, it must resort to some version of the essentialism it begins by repudiating."[121] Michaels sees constructionists as caught between two horns of a dilemma – given the constructionist argument: either race is voluntary (one chooses to belong to racial group X); or, race is essential. Michaels' identification argument can be constructed in the following manner.[122]

1.   Social constructionists hold that race is nothing but culture.
2.   Culture is nothing more than what we do and what we believe.
3.   Race is nothing more than what we do and what we believe.
4.   Therefore, to believe and practice what the members of any race believe or practice would, by definition, make one a member of that race.

The argument forces the social constructionist into an unsatisfactory conclusion. Given the Michaels argument and the phenomenon of *passing*, one must conclude that a) race is voluntary, and b) *passing* is impossible. But the claim by constructionism was that race is objective and *passing* is possible. This argument clearly provides a fundamental problem for racial constructionism in that the constructionist position claims that the ontological objectivity of race arises out of its inter-subjective nature given a society in a historical moment, or race is epistemically objective by the social conventions of a society. But if either position was correct, *passing* would be possible and race would not be voluntary, and the constructionist theory would be able to explicate the how and why of *passing* within its theoretical domain. So far, constructionism has failed to do so.

I agree with Michaels that the phenomenon of *passing* illustrates that the objectivity claimed by the constructionists is false. If race is given to an individual by the culture, *passing* would only be possible by the culture's granting a re-designation of a person's racial group. In such a way, the *passing* constraint would be fulfilled: race would be ontologically objective and *passing* possible. Upon reexamination, however, such a move makes race socially arbitrary and *passing* would no longer exist since a re-designation would allow a person to objectively be whatever racialized group a person chooses, thus undermining the power of strong social construction which, in turn, creates racial ambiguity. In the end, such a move defeats the constructionist claim for ontological objectivity.

The radical constructionist epistemic objectivity is also in trouble. If the individual's cognitive processes are determined by the social conventions and constructs of that society, then *passing* should be impossible. If it is true that I am what I have been designated, and my cognitive faculties are in line with social conventions (since all I know is a construction), then *passing* would not be an option for me. In the end, it looks as if constructionism has failed the *passing* constraint.

As a counter-argument, Mallon suggests that the Michaels' argument is wrongly cast. It assumes perceptual identification determines race.[123] Mallon quotes Gooding-Williams defense in writing, "constructionists may hold that race is nothing but culture in that practices of racial classification are nothing but culture, and that it is these practices that determine the criteria for racial membership."[124] For Michaels, this counter claim simply displaces the problem. The problem is, if one's race is a matter of how one is classified, and I am classified as Asian, then I am Asian.[125] But if this is the constructionist claim, once again it makes *passing* impossible. In this argument, classification is based on perception. If S looks black, S is black. So, if S acts black and looks black, and is classified as black, even if S is objectively white, S is black. Once again, the *passing* constraint is violated, and the constructionist argument becomes incoherent.

Mills attempts to substantiate his constructionist position in the following manner. I present his argument as the following:

1. Actual racial ascriptions are judgments about whether a person meets the relevant criteria to be a member of racial group X.
2. The criteria are the subject of an agreement of the community (society) as to what are the appropriate conditions for application.

A person's racial ascription by the community is a twofold project: 1) the community agrees upon the criteria for the application of racial labels; and 2) the community determines the race of an individual by reference to the agreed upon criteria. In support of the position of Mills, Mallon writes,

> Such an account allows us to understand how there could be objective but constructed facts about racial membership, and how particular judgments about racial membership could be genuinely wrong (as in the case of passing).
>
> To see how mere agreement on the criteria can create an objective category, consider the rules of baseball. The rules of baseball determine the batter's strike zone, and thereby determine for a given pitch, whether that pitch is a strike. It's because we recognize the rules as determining an objective fact about strikes that we can say things like 'the umpire made a bad call' – [W]e can make sense of a community being mistaken about a person's race just as we make sense of a strike in baseball – by reference to the antecedently agreed upon criteria that the community was attempting to apply.[126]

This is an interesting move by Mallon to save the constructionist theory from the problem of *passing*. So, like a baseball game, the rules are set as to balls and strikes. The activity is governed by the community representative (the umpire). If *passing* was about mistaken labeling (what is a ball and what a strike is), this analogy could save the constructionist position. But Mallon has committed the fallacy of apples and oranges. *Passing* would be more like a batter deciding that he wanted to play first base and then proceeding to the first base position, acting like a first baseman – when the rules say he is the batter. Again, *passing* must include an act of volition on the part of the person. What Mallon seems to be arguing is a case of mislabeling and calling it the phenomenon of *passing*. Mallon's recast of the argument misses the crux of the problem. The problem is again, how may one by the social constructionism concept of race account for the willful attempt of a person to "pass" for a member of another race and still maintain that race is objective? Mallon's analogy does not work in resolving this problem.

Mills suggests that the crux of the problem rests with understanding the nature of the criteria a community would use in applying race.[127]

Mills writes,

> I want to turn now to the question of the possible
> criteria for determining racial identity.... Seven possible
> candidates for racial self- and other-identification may
> be distinguished. They are not at all necessarily mutually
> exclusive, since they usually function in conjunction with
> one another. ... The categories are bodily appearance,
> ancestry, self-awareness of ancestry, public awareness of
> ancestry, culture, experience, and self-identification.[128]

Given this statement, one would ask, "Is there a priority in the
ranking of these categories of the criteria?" Mills response is that
the criteria are divided between indicative and central categories.[129]
A category is indicative, "... if having the property increases the
likelihood that one is a member of the category (i.e. race). A category
is central when:

> A criterion p for the application of a term or concept c is
> central to the extent that users of c consider p's obtaining
> to be a necessary or sufficient condition for the application
> of c. [130]

Given the above, the traditional constructionist response to
passing would be:

> Passing occurs when someone has the properties that
> are central to membership in one category but has other
> properties that are indicative of membership in another
> mutually exclusive category.[131]

It seems appropriate to ask at this point, "What categories are
central and what categories are indicative?" Who decides which
is which? It seems that we can deduce that the community, by
intersubjective relations and conventions, has determined the central
and indicative categories for an objective racial identity. And it looks
as if the constructionist concept of race has fulfilled the *passing*
constraint. However, when pressed further, what becomes a central
category for both the traditional constructionist and the radical

constructionist is the category of ancestry. Mills states, "… in the U. S. racial system, at least for whites and blacks, ancestry is taken as both necessary and sufficient for racial membership."[132] Taylor states, "… our races have in effect become breeding populations, which in turn means that there is some warrant for thinking of races as genetically distinct…."[133] Notice the comments of both the traditional and radical constructionist. "Ancestry" and "breeding populations" are central to membership in a race. But if the central category for membership is ancestry, how is this different from the essentialist claim that race is determined by "heritable characteristics, traits, and qualities?" It seems to me, without question, that Michaels is correct in his critique regarding the concept of race as a social construct. As he's quoted earlier in this chapter, "… it must resort to some version of the essentialism it begins by repudiating." Given the notion of central categories for the ascription of racial identity, we are once again left with an essentialist idea of race.

The thrust of this argument against race as a social construct is as follows.

1. Traditional and radical social constructionism fail as adequate concepts of race because neither can give credible evidence as to how race is objective (ontologically or epistemologically) and how the phenomenon of *passing* occurs. In the end, both camps must conclude that given the act of *passing*, race must be voluntary. But if race is voluntary, the ontological objective nature of race is lost. If *passing* is possible, then the epistemic objectivity is also.

2. The traditional and radical constructionists attempt to put together categories of indicative and central categories for racial identification. Both groups agree that ancestry is a central category of racial membership. But if ancestry is central to racial identity, then we have returned to a version of racial essentialism, which was the very concept social constructionism promised to defeat. For social constructionism to be able to a) explain *passing*, and b) have the ability to label rightly, a form of essentialism must be in play. If so, social constructionism is self-referentially incoherent.

It is clear that social constructionism has failed as an adequate concept of race. In the next chapter, we will investigate an anti-objectivist, nihilistic theory of race known as racial skepticism or racelessness. It is the complimentary position to traditional and radical constructionism. Racial skepticism was birthed in the school of social constructionism and is therefore fit for our investigation.

Chapter 4

RACIAL SKEPTICISM, RACIAL NIHILISM OR RACELESSNESS

Racial classifications have been imposed on us and our events solely through the racializing actions of the government, social science, and the media. But race does not exist.[134]

In Chapter 3, we were presented with a concept of race as a social construct with an objective status. This idea posits race is a social construct and race is real. According to this constructionist theory, the objective status of race is divided into two main categories.

The first category, traditional racial social constructionism (my term), as represented by Charles Mills, posits race as a phenomenon that is ontologically objective. Traditional social constructionism reasons that a social ontology is created by the intersubjective relationships that prevail within the contemporary socio-historical community in which we live. This position asserts that social constructs have the power to create social realities. If race is a social construct, racial realities also exist which, as social constructs, have the power to ascribe races and formulate racial classifications. Thus, racial classifications and, in turn, racial identities are real.

The socially established, ontologically objective reality of race is denoted by a set of criteria affirmed and supported by individuals within society. Racial classification, which in turn formulates racial identity, is not arbitrary. Racial classification, set by the social criteria, is sealed by the social ontological reality out of which it emerges. Mills formulates the criteria in the following manner:

> I want to turn now to the question of the possible criteria for determining racial identity... Seven possible candidates for racial self- and other- identification may be distinguished. They are not all necessarily mutually exclusive, since they usually function in conjunction with one another. The categories are bodily appearance, ancestry, self-awareness of ancestry, public awareness of ancestry, culture, experience, and self-identification. [135]

As the intersubjective relations of persons within a historical community create a social ontology that is real, the ontological character of race is real. Thus, race possesses an objective ontological status.

The second category of race under the objective social constructionist umbrella is the claim that race is objective (has social ontology) and epistemological (knowable to a person). This position is designated as radical racial social constructionism. The radical racial social constructionist position maintains that race is objectively real not because of an existent social ontology, but because its objectivity is grounded in an epistemological reality generated by the social conventions of a historical community. The conventions, which are fixed by the practice, affirmation, and tradition of members of the historical community, determine our noetic structures in such a way that social constructs have a reality (e.g. money) that is agreed upon by a community and independent of individual fiat.

The social constructs in the epistemic mode of thinking serve as the categories of our understanding. They determine not only what we cognize, but also how our noetic processes function. What the social constructs determine is what is epistemically permissible and what is not permissible. Regarding race, the racial classifications ascribe race socially, but permeate our noetic framework in such a manner that our thinking confirms race as an objective epistemological reality. So, for the radical race constructionist, race is ontologically subjective (because there are no natural kinds to which race denotes) but epistemologically objective and therefore real.

A summary of the objective social constructionist's argument:

1. In our culture, strong social constructs exist and are taken for granted by members of this (U.S.) culture.
2. Race is a strong social construct.
3. Social constructs possess the quality of appearing inevitable.
4. Social constructs need not exist in their present form.
5. Social constructs are not inevitable.
6. Strong social constructs, including race, are objectively real.
7. Race as a social construct is ontologically real, based on our social ontology (the traditional position).
8. Race is epistemologically real based on our social conventions (the radical position).
9. Therefore, race is real.

What we discovered in Chapter 3 was that the concept of race as a social construct with objective reality failed when confronted by two problematic phenomena: social racial mislabeling (the "Pudd'nhead Wilson Syndrome") and the intentional practice of *passing*. Neither the traditional nor radical positions can adequately address what the nature of race is, given the phenomena of mislabeling and/or *passing*. Given these phenomena, either race is determined by culture (what we do and what we believe) or by ancestry (which is bloodlines). If race is determined by culture, then anyone can be any race and to speak of races makes no sense. If race is determined by ancestry, then we are back to a form of racial essentialism. Since the objective constructionist positions cannot handle the mislabeling phenomenon or the *passing* constraint, we must, therefore, reject the concept of race as a social construct with an objective status.

This chapter will examine a different idea of race as a social construct. The position next selected for examination is called racial nihilism or racial skepticism or, by some, "racelessness." Throughout the course of this chapter, I will use these terms interchangeably. Racial nihilism/skepticism believes "… race talk is at best an egregious error, and at worst a pernicious lie."[136] Racial skepticism is currently advocated in many sections of academia and by a few spokespersons within the populace. I will focus on two of the position's most vocal and prominent advocates, although other proponents of racial nihilism will also be used in this section. The two main persons are Kwame Anthony Appiah and Naomi Zack. What is the motivation of advocating racial nihilism? At this point we turn our attention to the argument for this position that race is a social construct with no objective status. From this point on I shall use the terms racial skepticism and racial nihilism for this anti-objective concept of race.

The Argument for Racial Skepticism

> Instead of obsessing about race, we could try to build a [raceless] race-blind society. Instead of feeding the fires of neuroticism, we could start teaching people to forget about race, to move on. But to do that, first we must sideline the entire race relations industry – whose only function, it seems, is to make us all deeply anxious about 'race' – a concept they simultaneously believe has no objective reality. [137]

When one thinks about the current debate about race and the seemingly irresolvable nature of the discussion, perhaps the best thing to do is to "move on" and admit that the objective character of race is dubious at best. The general argument for racial nihilism is constructed in the following manner.

1. In our culture, strong social constructs exist and are taken for granted by members of this society.
2. All social constructs are the invention of human communities of a historical period.
3. Social constructs did not have to exist or exist in the manner they appear within a historical community.
4. Though social constructs appear inevitable, they are not inevitable.
5. Race is a social construct.

6. There is no scientific evidence for the existence of races.
7. Racial ascriptions have no objective reality because they are social constructs void of scientific evidence and are the products of human historical communities.
8. Therefore, races are not real.

A preliminary analysis of the argument reveals racial nihilism's similarity and dissimilarity to racial objective social constructionism. Premises 1-5 demonstrate the similarity to the objective position. For both positions, race is a strong social construct, has the character of inevitability, and is the product of human historical communities. The dissimilarity emerges when premises 6 and 7 are stated. These two premises focus the arguments against the existence of race both positively and negatively.[138]

The positive side of the racial nihilist argument is that for the sake of racial harmony, social progress, and mutual justice, it implores us to transcend prior racial identity politics, racial ontologies, and race classification. Such a plea makes us reflect upon how deceptive and destructive racial discourse has been. Racial reasoning may have provided a foundation for communal solidarity for racialized groups in the past, but now it only fractures the human community and creates an oppressive racial consciousness for members of racialized groups.[139]

The negative aspect of the racial skepticism argument posits that race concepts are neither scientifically verifiable nor biologically factual. In summarizing the racial nihilist argument, John Shuford writes,

> Race concepts and racial identities [for racial nihilists] are impediments to self- and collective emancipation that are fictitious and overburdened with historical and conceptual baggage. If race and racial definitions are arbitrary...then with concerted effort we might be able to transcend race, racial definitions, and racial injustice.[140]

The positive yearning to transcend racial ontological formations coupled with the negative assertion that racial concepts operate by faulty biology motivate the racial nihilist position. Now we move attention to racial nihilism's biological argument against the existence of races

A Biological Argument against the Existence of Race

Appiah and Zack heavily lean on the lack of bio-genetic verification of race. Both suggest that recent bio-genetic technological research has demonstrated that race is relatively unimportant in explaining human variation. Appiah and Zack state that there clearly exists no causal relationship between race and intellectual or moral capacity. Appiah writes:

> Every reputable biologist will agree that human genetic variability between the populations of Africa or Europe or Asia is not much greater than that within those populations, though how much greater depends, in part, on the measure of genetic variability the biologist chooses. If biologists want to make interracial difference seem relatively large, they can say that "the proportion of genic variation attributable to racial difference is ...91.1%." ... If they want to make it seem small, they can say that, for two people who are both "Caucasoid," the chances of differing in genetic constitution at one site on a given chromosome have recently been estimated at about 14.3 percent, while for any two people taken at random from the human population the same calculations suggest a figure about 14.8 percent. The underlying statistical facts about the distribution of variant characteristics in human populations and subpopulations are the same, whichever way you express the matter.
>
> I can now express simply one measure of the extent to which members of those human populations we call races differ more from each other than they do from members of the same race. For the value J for "Caucasoid" – estimated, in fact, largely from samples of the English population – is estimated to be about 0.857, while that for the whole human population is estimated at 0.852. The chances, in other words, that two people taken at random from the human population will have the same characteristic at a random locus are about 85.2 percent, while the chances for

two (white) people taken from the population of England are about 85.7 percent. And since 85.2 is 100 minus 14.8, and 85.7 is 100 minus 14.3, this is equivalent to what I said previously: the chances of two people who are both "Caucasoid" differing in genetic constitution at one site on a given chromosome are about 14.3 percent, while, for any two people taken at random from the human population, they are about 14.8 percent.

The conclusion is obvious: given only a person's race, it is hard to say what his or her biological characteristics will be.[141]

Given the above conclusion we may further conclude that since our genetic constitutions are so similar, and given the ambiguity between our biological characteristics and race, race is bio-genetically unverifiable and therefore "relatively unimportant in explaining biological differences between people."[142] Appiah goes on to suggest that there are good reasons for concluding that large portions of the human community will not fit into ascribed racial classes if the criteria are bio-genetically based.[143] The only feature of human characteristics that seems to be tied to genetics is morphology and that logical fact, Appiah believes, is a poor way of classifying the human community:

> To say that biological races existed because it was possible to classify people into a small number of classes according to their gross morphology would be to save racialism in the letter but lose it in the substance. The notion of race that was recovered would be of no biological interest ... We can just as well classify people according to whether or not they were redheaded, or redheaded and freckled, or redheaded, freckled, and broad-nosed too, but nobody claims that this sort of classification is central to human biology [or to the objective reality of races].[144]

Appiah's argument against concepts of race and subsequent race-consciousness identity theories lead him to three fundamental conclusions.

1. Essentialist and social ontological (including epistemological) concepts of race assume the reality of race rather than

exposing the fictitious and arbitrary nature of racial concepts. Such assumptions lead us to conceptual commitments that in the least are false and at most are racist and dangerous.

2. Most concepts of race rely on sociohistorical accounts that are historically and conceptually erroneous. Appiah rejects the idea of a shared Africana (i.e. Africa and its Diaspora) racial identity or racial experience. Appiah writes, "[W]e do not have a common traditional culture, common languages, [and] a common religious or conceptual vocabulary. We do not even belong to a common race."[145]

3. The continued attempts of racial theorists to fashion a positive communal racial identity based on a faulty biology thwarts our necessary socio-political need for transcendence of racial categories.

Appiah remarks:

> Race, we all assume, is, like all other concepts, constructed by metaphor and metonymy; it stands in, metonymically, for the Other; it bears the weight, metaphorically, of other kinds of difference.
>
> Yet, in our social lives away from the text-world of the academy, we take reference for granted too easily. Even if the concept of race is a structure of oppositions ... it is a structure whose realization is, at best, problematic and, at worst impossible. The truth is that there are no races; there is nothing in the world that can do all we ask "race" to do for us. The evil that is done is done by the concept [of race] and by easy – yet impossible – assumptions as to its application. What we miss through our obsession with the structure of relations of concepts is, simply, reality.[146]

Reality demands, according to the advocate of the racial skepticism position, that we transcend essentialist and objective concepts of race, moving onward to the freedom of "race-less-ness."

It must be noted that the above statements of Appiah reflect an earlier idea in his thinking. Currently, Appiah has shifted his philosophical thinking from racial nihilism to a racial nominalist position. But the earlier statement demonstrates the importance the biological evidence has for the racial skepticism position. The question, simply put, asks, is race a useful characterization to describe human biological variation? The proponent of racial nihilism unabashedly state, "No."

The racial nihilist position entails other ideas regarding race [e.g. issues of privilege and power] which affect social life. It encourages us to neglect most of the many respects in which people are different or alike, most of the many grounds we've given ourselves for treating [people of different races] less well than we otherwise might.[147] Taylor concludes by stating, "All of this is to say: our Western races are social constructs. They are things that we humans create in the transactions that define social life."[148] How the racial nihilist differs from a radical constructionist is that the nihilist believes that since race is a social construct, it necessarily means that race is not real. D. Marvin Jones writes, "… racial categories are neither objective nor natural, but ideological and constructed. In these terms race is not so much a category but a practice: people are raced."[149]

In concert with Appiah, Naomi Zack also rejects theories of race that are essentialist or socially objective in nature. Like Appiah, Zack leans on the biological issue regarding race. Zack writes:

> The average American, and many scholars as well, still believe that there is some coherent biological basis for the racial categories of black, white, Indian and Asian, and that relevant scientists have specialized information about the nature of that basis. Race, however, is a social construction on all levels. Not only are the links between so-called biological race and culture the result of history, tradition, and current norms, but the existence of biological taxonomies is itself the result of such social factors. If human races existed, then more people would be properly described as mixed race than are commonly thought to be. But, since human biological race is a fiction, so is mixed race.[150]

Zack's racial nihilism is an attempt to form a holistic and emancipatory concept of identity which she believes is thwarted by the adherence to biological race. For Zack, adherence to the former concepts of race (which she calls *the ordinary concept of race*) is irrational, absent of empirical veracity, and racist.

> Black and white racial designations are themselves racist because the concept of race does not have an adequate scientific foundation. If racial designations are racist, then people ought not to be identified in the third person as members of races, then individuals in the first person ought not to have racial identities.[151]

Her objection is that the "designations" of race are grounded on "[the practice] that when an individual is designated black or white, the individual has some physical characteristics and does not have some other physical characteristics – the ordinary concept of race purports to refer to an individual's body." The subsequent categorization of black and white is not equal in value, social hierarchy, or content. Zack insists that black refers to both race and ethnicity; the latter is dependent on the former. Black is clouded with negative images, while white is held as purity of lineage, positive value and social recognition by whites as "white."[152] The delineation of races rests on the "kinship schema of racial inheritance" or the "one drop rule," but not biological truth.

> There is nothing in the world to which the term' black' refers in the bodies of all individuals to whom that term is applied.... [T]he kinship system does not rest on any scientific facts about race, because there are no scientific facts about race that support the ordinary concept of race.[153]

Therefore, for Zack, racial categories do not exist. Since there are no racial essences, or categories of racial classification supported by scientific facts, or necessary and sufficient conditions for membership in a race, the term race is without meaning.

The practice of racial classification is racist for Zack for three main reasons.[154]

1. Racial classification automatically excludes some people from white identity and culture even if they have white ancestors. If

racial classification employs ancestry as a criterion for racial classification, and given the fact that all people are of mixed racial ancestry, why are those of a different morphology automatically excluded?

2. Racial categorizations and identity ascriptions reinforce beliefs in white supremacy by making whiteness and/or being white something of value, and a property that others cannot have.

3. Racial classifications force "mixed raced" persons to identify with one race over and against the other race. They must choose either a race that has been socially imposed or devalued or participate in *passing* at the exclusion of members of a racial group, which in turn causes existential angst and interpersonal cost.

As a result, Zack embraces the disassociation of people from racial classification, and urges us to adopt the position of racial nihilism. Zack asserts:

> I refuse to be pressured into denying the existence of black forbearers to please whites, and I refuse to be pressured into denying white ethnicity and my white forbearers, to please blacks. There is no biological foundation for the concept of race. The concept of race is an oppressive cultural invention and convention, and I refuse to have anything to do with it. I refuse to be reasonable to placate either blacks or whites who retain non-empirical and irrational categorizations. Therefore, I have no racial affiliation and will accept no racial designations.[155]

The Argument against Racial Skepticism

While the arguments presented by the earlier thinking of Appiah, and currently by Zack, are compelling on the surface, a closer examination requires that we must reject racelessness for two fundamental reasons. The first reason is that contrary to the claim of racial skepticism that there are no biological races, modern genetic research states there is a biological foundation for race. I will demonstrate that the argument of racial nihilism is counterfactual to current bio-genetic findings. The second reason I argue against racial skepticism is that it denies the veracity of the lived experiences of race for racialized people. I will present the full arguments sequentially.

I. The Argument of a Biological Foundation of Race

The proponents of racelessness are correct that race, given a nineteenth-century biological conceptualization is inaccurate. The science of that time attempted not only to provide us with evidence of a racial essence inherent to races, it also attempted to demonstrate that given such a racial essence, we could predict with a high degree of certainty the intellectual ability and moral capacity of racial groups and their members. The nineteenth-century scientific claims, matched with Hegel's philosophical racial hierarchy, gave rise in the early twentieth century to Social Darwinism and the racial characterizations associated with it. The horrific historical episode of racial subjugation that transpired during that era, and persists even to this day, has caused philosophers to reject any notion of a biological foundation for race. If the current bio-genetic data is simply a recapitulation of the nineteenth century's racial essentialism, then the argument for racial nihilism would be warranted. However, such is not the case.

The current scientific data states that there exists a genetic profile such that race can be identified and indicated based on genetic information. The genetic racial profile is based on gene formation, sequential placement, and temporal locations with the genetic information combined with allele matching; conclusive indicators of human variation can be racially marked. How the contemporary genetic claim is distinguished from the nineteenth century model is that the current genetic information in no way attempts to suggest racially determined intellect or the moral agency of races. It simply states that as complex neuro-physiological organisms, human racial variations are bio-genetically grounded and not merely social constructions. The current genetic research simply attempts to state physiologically *what we are, not who we are.* The "what we are" is only what we are as physical entities in the world. The genetic description in no way attempts to embrace a racial hierarchy as was the project of nineteenth and early twentieth century biological concepts of race. Current geneticists agree that we create the "who we are" by the exercise of will, response to environment, historical influence, family of origin, and the like. Clearly there is a qualitative difference between the strong racial biology of the nineteenth and early twentieth centuries and the weak bio-genetic asserts of today.

There is credible scientific evidence for the existence of races.

> Research in the last 35 years has uncovered significant differences among racial and ethnic groups in their rates of drug metabolism, in clinical responses to drugs, and in drug side effects. African-American and White patients differ significantly in their responses to beta-blockers, ACE inhibitors, and diuretics used either alone or in combination for the treatment of hypertension. Chinese are considerably more sensitive than Whites to the effects of the beta-blocker propranolol on heart rate and blood pressure. A clear message of the recent findings in this field is that racial and ethnic differences must be factored into formulary selection and prescribing decisions....[156]

This evidence has given rise to bio-racial drugs such as Actonel which cannot be successfully used by Latino and Africana female populations but is used by Asian and Caucasian women for the prevention and treatment of osteoporosis.[157] The production and prescription of these drugs considered differences in social-economic factors that previously thwarted attempts at bio-racial medicines. The success of the current bio-racial medicines is supported by genetic information and metabolic differences among races and not merely sociological factors such as class limitations in diet, food supply, or environmental conditions as once thought. A clear case of a weak genetic link to races is the successful use of Lumigan for the treatment of glaucoma in African Americans but is overwhelmingly unsuccessful in the treatment of glaucoma with other racial populations.[158]

The evidence influences medical instances such as bone marrow transplants and the treatment of racially determined diseases such as sickle cell anemia. In each case the evidence seems to suggest that race is a factor in treatment. What is the philosophical impact of the new evidence?

Previously, there was no argument other than nineteenth century essentialism that dared to make a connection between race and biology, thus the claims of philosophers like Zack seemed plausible. Arguments for the reality of race were vested in the context of objective social constructionism. Now, however, given the current genetic research it is credible to construct the following argument.

1. The human species is divided into various genetic groups.
2. The variation between groups is genetically caused.
3. Race is a genetic code for human variations.
4. The human bio-genetic formations are descriptive of certain physiological (racial) variations and metabolic traits, but do not determine a racial group's intellectual ability or moral capacity.
5. The genetic formations constitute a weak biological foundation for racial distinctions.
6. Race, therefore, does have a biological foundation.
7. Therefore, racial skepticism is false.

Two points of consideration need to be expressed. First, the above argument does not take into consideration the social and political implications of race. One could argue that race has as much (or more) to do with privilege and power as it does with biology, and that to discount this fact gives us a skewed perception of race.[159] It is true that race has social and political implications. But we must be careful in trying to make a theory do too much. The discussion of the social and political aspects of race belongs to our meta-narrative about race. What I believe that science is doing is simply giving us a descriptive account of race grounded in physiology. No scientific (including social scientific) description can ever be the end of the story regarding humanity. Philosophers must provide the analytic and prescriptive meta-narratives if our total description is to be complete.

The second point is more mundane. The reason the genetic information is important is that it provides us with the necessary counter evidence to defeat racial skepticism. Zack and others are simply wrong in their insistence that race is false. If there was no evidence of a biological foundation to race, racial nihilism would be correct. But, since there is credible evidence supporting a biological link to racial variations, racelessness is wrong; Q.E.D.

The philosophical hesitation to commit to a biological foundation of race comes from a remembrance of the atrocities that occurred in our history with past nineteenth and early twentieth century ideas of racial hierarchy and Social Darwinism. The result of earlier attempts at establishing biological race has left an indelible mark upon the American social psyche. No one can forget the horrors that have occurred because of *race talk* in general and biological *race talk* in particular. There is the worry that the new biology will become the victim of the "slippery slope" dilemma: Biological race configuration will lead to biological racism. Taylor notes this problem when he writes:

> The history of [biological] race-thinking does provide ample motivation for the slippery slope worry. The modern world has been irrevocably and tragically shaped by race-related oppression, exclusion, exploitation, and genocide. And even if we could somehow guarantee that there would be no more large-scale, world-historical tragedies like the Holocaust … the notion of [biological] race would still make possible all the small-scale exclusions and slights that can poison the atmosphere of daily life.
>
> Looking back at the history of race–thinking does reveal these and other ethical problems. But if we look forward to the continuing need to traverse the social terrain that's been shaped by racially motivated wrongs and tragedies, we may find it more useful to hold on to race than to abolish it.[160]

I agree with Taylor on this point. Just because X (with X being exploitation, subjugation, genocide, etc.) has been the case in the past regarding early notions of biological race, that does not mean that X will be the case in the future. I hold out for a humanity whose rational capacity, matched with a passionate sense of justice, can avoid horrors we have experienced in our common history. To refuse to accept the new data because of past errors is to commit epistemological hamartia. Because biological race has been the basis of irresponsible conduct in the past, historical failings cannot be used as a sufficient argument to discount the new theory of biological race. I want to believe that given the horrors of our racial history the chances of perversion of the new theory of biological race are greatly diminished. We are creatures that can learn our lessons from the past, though sometimes slowly.

The weak (i.e. weak in the philosophical sense) formation of a genetic link to race avoids the previous problems of ranking racial groups and subsequently demeaning of a race's intellectual and/ or capacity. It simply notes the existence of genetically verifiable differences in the human variation (races) but makes no evaluative statement regarding racial potential either individually or corporately.

Therefore, given a preponderance of the evidence for a biological foundation to race, we must conclude that racial skepticism is false.

II. The Incomplete Argument for the "Lived Experience" of Race

The whole history of the Negro is tragic. By what accursed violation did they first exist that they should suffer always...they never go out without being insulted.

Ralph Waldo Emerson
Journal, August 25, 1838

I maintain that even if there were no scientific evidence for the existence of race, race is real. My argument is based on the lived experiences of racialized people who live in a concrete historical community and are confronted by the reality of racism. Everyday racialized people are cognizant of the power and reality of race. The phenomenological reality of race is unavoidable. Every aspect of human personality of the racialized person is affected. I will say more about this phenomenon in the next section, but here I wish only to give descriptive evidence of the fact: race is real.

The reality of race is demonstrated in the social interactions of members of a historical community. The history of American society gives credence to this claim. The non-inclusion of African Americans in the Declaration of Independence because African Americans were only three-fifths human, the genocidal activity against Amerindians in the westward expansion, and the internment of Japanese Americans all point to the fact: race is real and has been a major part of social interaction for a long time.

The historical activities stated, and the numerous others not stated, did not occur in a vacuum. They resulted from laws enacted by a historical community with a racial group in mind. The laws were upheld by the social constructs we created and codified by our social conventions. This is not an episode of cheap finger-pointing. I am merely suggesting that the result of the above activity had real effects on the lives of real people. They did not imagine their oppression and subjugation; their tears and sorrows were not an illusion. For racial nihilism to claim that race is not real is to state, by association, that the lived experiences of the victims of race are not real. That conclusion I find absurd.

The counter-argument from racial skepticism could be that all the above accounts are of a past era draped in a fictitious understanding of human variety. 'We are a more intellectually sophisticated people now. The tragedy of slavery is over. There are no more Jim Crow laws. The Civil Rights Movement has brought about an epistemic shift in our thinking. Racism is over, and thus the reality of race has ended.'

In response to this kind of thinking, Cornel West writes:

> [T]he vicious legacy of white supremacy has inflicted deeper wounds on the American landscape. These deep wounds provide a profound lens – they yield painful truths about the limits of democracy in America. The sentimental flight from history – or adolescent escape from painful truths about ourselves – means that even as we grow old, grow big, and grow powerful, we have yet to grow up. To confront the role of race…is to grapple with what we would like to avoid, but we avoid that confrontation at the risk of our democratic maturation.[161]

Maturity demands two things. First, it demands that we understand that while de jure racism is non-existent, de facto racism is a reality in the American democratic experiment. Reflection upon the tragedy of Hurricane Katrina and Mr. Bush's response, the recent execution of "Tookie" Williams, the growing nihilism in African American and Latino communities in this country forces us to realize that race is a powerful factor and real presence in our contemporary lives. The struggle to create a racially pluralistic society continues. The story of lived experiences of African Americans, for instance, is a story of the lived experiences of race and the struggle for a truly democratic community. It is a story that often is told in music and poetry, emergent from the lived experiences of real people. James Baldwin states:

> It is only in his music, which Americans can admire because a protective sentimentality limits their understanding of it, that the Negro in America has been able to tell his story. It is a story which otherwise has yet to be told and which no American is prepared to hear....
>
> The story of the Negro is the story of America – or, more precisely, it is the story of Americans. It is not a very pretty story: the story of a people is never very pretty.[162]

Maturity also demands that we must take seriously the lived experiences of race for the millions of people who are subjected to it every day. The power of institutionalized racism has had a destructive effect on racialized people in America. Race has fundamentally impacted the rate of Black on Black crime and the rise of AIDS in Africana and Latino communities around the world. Racelessness refuses to take the lives of the racialized American minority/majority into account. For that reason, racial skepticism must be utterly rejected.

A second and adjacent counter-argument against the reality of race from lived experience suggests that racial thinking, grounded in lived experiences, has a way of causing people to imagine their lives in narrow modes. The reality of race by experience can create a stifling framework in which individuality is stifled. Taylor casts the racial nihilist argument thusly:

> [Another] ethical complaint against [experiential] race thinking is that it encourages individuals to envision their life plans in overly narrow ways. It encourages them to think of themselves, their prospects, their personal styles, and their relationships in accordance with oppressive racial scripts.[163]

My response at this point is simply that past events always tell me two things: how I am seen by others (i.e. my social identity) and how I see myself (personal identity). My personal identity, while shaped by my experiences and my social identity, can never determine the "who I am." Personal identity is a matter of choice, sometimes despite what others think or project that I am. More will be said about the dual nature of identity in the next chapter. But for now, I posit that lived experiences of race provide the opportunity to rise above and create the fundamentally new. Every occasion of self-realization is comprised of the threat of annihilation and the hope of self-actualization. Personal value and self-worth must be the result of one's own creative initiative. Past experiences, personal and corporate, show not only that the task of creating value and worth for one's self must be done, it shows that it can be done. Toni Morrison writes:

> Those people could not live without value. They had prices, but no value in the white world, so they made their own, and they decided what was valuable. It was usually eleemosynary, usually something they were doing for somebody else. Nobody…no adult black person, survives by self-regard, narcissism, [or] selfishness. They took the sense of community for granted. It never occurred to them they could live outside of it.[164]

Thus, the racial skeptic's claim that "lived experiences" stifle individuality by narrowing life plans and goals lacks warrant. It may be the case that individuals have allowed past events to trap their creative vision for themselves and their children, but there is nothing inherent in lived experiences that necessarily suffocate human ingenuity. The choice of who we are is always left with us. Racial skepticism must be applauded in its attempt to move beyond past constructions of race and racial classifications. I believe that the goal of racial skeptics is to create a "beloved community" where race does not matter. Such efforts are to be commended. But the racial skeptics, in their attempt to move beyond racial designations that thwart human progress, overlook crucial biological facts and discount important personal narratives. The racial skeptics have the right vision, just the wrong methodology.

In this chapter, the argument for racial skepticism, racial nihilism, or racelessness has been presented. The position is a powerful one that for many has been persuasive. Yet, given new advancements in genetic research, along with the affirmation of the lived experiences of racialized people, we must in good conscience reject the racial skeptic's position. In the next chapter, I will focus more on the idea of lived experience and how it is the foundation for an existential/phenomenological concept of race.

Chapter 5

RACE AS AN EXISTENTIAL PROCESS

I must take the responsibility for how, mark my word, how I react to
the forces that impinge upon my life, forces that are not responsive
to my will, my desire, my ambition, my dream, my hope – forces
that don't know I'm here. And I decide whether I will say yes,
or no, and make it hold. This indeed is the free man, and this
is anticipated in the genius of the dogma of freedom...[165]

In this chapter we will investigate the final concept of race for this project. The focus of this chapter will be upon the concept of race as an existential-phenomenological process. But first, I shall review the conclusions of Chapter 4.

In Chapter 4 we examined the concept of race as a social construct with no status. This concept of race is commonly referred to as racial skepticism, racial nihilism, or racelessness. Race, according to this position, is non-existent for two fundamental reasons: first, because the nineteenth century biological evidence used to support the existence of races by racial essences proved fallacious. Evidence for biological race cannot be employed to support a belief in the existence of races:

A rough characterization has it that [racial nihilists] want to eliminate 'race' talk quickly... For example, Naomi Zack argues that the ordinary concept of race in the United States has no scientific basis, and K. Anthony Appiah insists that there are no races: there is nothing in the world that can do all we ask 'race' to do for us. According to Zack and Appiah, race talk makes reference to a set of racial properties that literally do not exist.[166]

Racial nihilists go on to suggest that even the twentieth century advancements in scientific (i.e. genetic) technology are of no help in giving clear and undeniable racial designations. Since no clear scientific evidence can be found for the existence of races, racial nihilists claim that races do not exist.

The second reason of the racial nihilist argument is that race must be thought of as a social construct. Since social constructs are not real, then race, as a social construct, is a fiction: Race is a social construction without empirical (i.e. scientific) verification. The history of racial essentialism and race as a social construct is so full of abuses of privilege and power against people of color that discarding the entire notion of race will be of benefit for society. Perhaps, say the racial skeptics, if we can get beyond race, we can create a post-racial community "where people are judged by the content of their character and not by the color of their skin."[167] In the first instance, to hold a belief in the existence of races is scientifically unjustified and analogous to belief in the Easter Bunny. In the second case, given the history of racism in the modern era to hold a belief in races is epistemologically and ethically abhorrent.

The motivation for racial nihilism is laudable. The history of racism in this country demonstrates clearly how a belief in racial essences can be perverted. From racial essentialism and the subsequent development of racial hierarchies, which was also derived from race as a social construct with objective status, came support for the classification of African Americans as non-human, three-fifths of a person, as well as justification of slavery, savage lynchings, rapes, and a host of horrors too gruesome to recall. The negative classification of races that developed gave access to privilege and power for people of European descent and the subjugation of other non-white races.

Racial essentialism and the social construction of race as real has been the impetus of oppression and disenfranchisement for non-white people (and those considered non-white such as Jews) throughout the history of this country. It has torn the fabric of our democratic republic and threatened our very existence as a society.[168] Therefore, racial skeptics keep the hope of a true democratic society, utopian in nature, before us. And for that we applaud the motivation and critical analysis of the racial skeptics.

While the descriptive analysis of the racial skeptics is correct, their conclusion is problematic. Countering the argument for racial nihilism, the following must be considered. First, contemporary biogenetics does suggest that races are biologically real in the weak sense. Genetics can designate race by allele construction. The presence of racially designated bio-medicines, racially specific bone marrow transplants, and treatment of glaucoma based on racial descriptions point to the fact that human variations can be determined raciogenetically. Race has a physiological link in the weak sense, in that it can demonstrate morphology and neurophysiological traits, but biological race does not influence intellectual ability or moral capacity. Given this new information, racial skepticism is false.

It may also be argued that – even without the new genetic evidence that establishes the existence of races in the weak sense – racelessness is a problematic philosophical position because it denies the authenticity of the lived experiences of racial groups and their members. Given the social ontology that each of us experience, race is a socially ontological reality. As such, racialized persons experience racial realities that cannot be dismissed. The experiences of people who are the victims of racism are not imagined. Racial skepticism diminishes the reality of race experiences, which in turn invalidates the lives of racialized people. For this second reason, the conclusion of racial nihilism must be rejected.

Now we turn our attention to the concept of race as an existential/phenomenological process. This position has gained growing support recently, primarily through the re-examination of such individuals as Jean Paul Sartre, Frantz Fanon, and contemporary philosopher Lewis R. Gordon. First, we examine the main tenets of existentialism.

A Preliminary Review of Existentialism

Existentialism emerged on the philosophical scene as a response to the Western rationalist tradition that began with Descartes. It distinguished itself from the rationalist position in two basic ways. **First**, it rejected the idea that reality is fundamentally rational consciousness. Descartes, in the *Meditations*, suggested that everything could be thought away except for three clear and distinct ideas: rational consciousness, God, and objects of the external world. Descartes states that by rational illumination, these can be "[seen] utterly [and] clearly with my mind's eye."[169] The reality of these clear and distinct ideas is more certain than any other reality. These are clear and distinct ideas which Descartes is certain cannot be products of his imagination. About his own existence as rational consciousness Descartes writes:

> I have convinced myself that there is absolutely nothing in the world, no sky, no earth, no minds, no bodies. Does it now follow that I too do not exist? No: if I convinced myself of something then I certainly existed. But there is a deceiver of supreme power and cunning who is deliberately and constantly deceiving me. In that case I too undoubtedly exist, if he is deceiving me; and let him deceive me as much as he can, he will never bring it about that I am nothing so long as I think that I am something. So after considering everything very thoroughly, I must finally conclude that this proposition, *I am, I exist,* is necessarily true whenever it is put forward by me or conceived in my mind.[170]

Of the existence of a God that is not a deceiver, and the external world Descartes writes:

> I have perceived that God exists, and at the same time I have understood that everything else depends on him, and that he is no deceiver; and I have drawn the conclusion that everything, which I clearly and distinctly perceive is of necessity true. ...what objections can now be raised? That the way I am made makes me prone to frequent error? But I now know that I am incapable of error in those cases where my understanding is transparently clear. ...And now it is

> possible for me to achieve full and certain knowledge of
> countless matters, both concerning God himself and other
> things whose nature is intellectual, and also concerning
> the whole of that corporeal nature which is the subject
> matter of pure mathematics.[171]

By the method of hyperbolic doubt, Descartes can come to absolute certainty of clear and distinct ideas. Notice that his certainty regarding the self, the world, and God rests upon the fact that they are ideas that cannot be created by imagination. Thus, for rationalism in the Cartesian form, the world of affairs is secondary to the world of clear and distinct ideas.

Instead, existentialism posed that, as conscious beings, we find ourselves in a world of prior context and history that cannot be thought away. For existentialism, the context in which we live and the history of the lived world is inextricably tied to conscious being. A person cannot detach from the actual world of affairs and be said to live in good faith. To do so, for existentialism, is to live in bad faith. Thus, ultimate reality is, in the words of Heidegger, "being in the world."[172]

Secondly, existentialism rejects the objective ontological notion of Aristotelian and Thomistic nominalism in reference to what it means to be human. Nominalism argued that the metaphysical constitution of humans posed an essence or nature that determined the moral capacity of people in such a way that one's capacity was determined absolutely by one's nature. If essence precedes existence, then one had no choice in the type of person one could be. Aristotle was clear that right being is being in accordance to essence.

> There is knowledge of each thing only when we know its
> essence. [For instance] that to which the essence of good
> does not belong is not good. The good, then, must be
> one with the essence of good, and the beautiful with the
> essence of beauty, and so with all things ... Each thing
> itself, then, and its essence are one and the same ...to know
> each thing, at least, is just to know its essence ....[173]

Existentialists objected to nominalism's description of human beings and argued that human freedom was lost if a person's ontological state was pre-determined by essence. Given the nominalist position, a person is totally determined by her nature; thus, moral agency is eradicated, and ethical decision-making is ultimately impossible.

Existentialism's motto became "existence precedes essence." In other words, first I exist and then my choices in existence determine what kind of being I become. Kierkegaard, who is considered by many as the father of existentialism, emphasized this point by demanding "truth is subjectivity." By this he meant that as human beings we can only be understood in terms of our lived experiences and the reality of them, which includes our dilemmas. What Kierkegaard and other existentialists object to is the attempt to understand the human condition from scientific descriptions or abstract philosophical notions of human nature. Samuel E. Stumpf, articulating the idea that truth is subjectivity, writes:

> By this strange notion he meant that there is no prefabricated truth "out there" for people who make choices. As American philosopher William James similarly said, **"truth is made" by an act of will**. For Kierkegaard, what is "out there" is only objective uncertainty.[174]

With existentialism, when considering the human condition, the premier question is what should be our starting point? Should it be our scientific notions, our philosophical or theological ideas regarding human nature, or some other starting point? Jean Paul Sartre suggests:

> Our point of departure is the subjectivity of the individual (the individual regarded as a subject who thinks, not as an object thought about). It is because we seek to base our teaching upon the truth. Any doctrine of probabilities, which is not attached to a truth, will crumble. To define the probable, one must possess the true. And there is such a truth. At the point of departure there cannot be any other truth than this: "I think, therefore I am." This theory does not begin by taking man as an object but as a subject.[175]

Undoubtedly, the contribution of existentialism to philosophy is the idea that each person's identity is constituted neither by nature, God, nor culture but by the creation of one's self and taking full responsibility for our choices.

From the above existential notions come three key ideas. They are facticity, alienation, and authenticity. Facticity refers to all the ways in which a person can establish identity from a third person perspective. These include natural characteristics such as weight, height, and morphology. They can also be social properties such as nationality and class. The issue for existentialism is that facticity is too often used by individuals to predicate the "what I am" as opposed to the individual exercising choice in the creating of "who I am."

Sartre classifies choosing to live by facticity as living *en soi* (in self), and he calls the exercise of our freedom to create self as living *pour soi* (for self).[176] Each person, in the existential framework, has the option of which way she will live. Existentialism, however, claims that to live in the third person mode or by facticity is an exercise of bad faith. Facticity cannot define or clearly articulate the type that I am. Thus, existentialism urges the individual to adapt an attitude of transcendence. Steven Cowell writes;

> Transcendence refers to that attitude toward myself characteristic of my practical engagement in the world, the agent's perspective. An agent is oriented by the task at hand as something to be brought about through its own will or agency... To speak of 'transcendence' here is to indicate that the agent "goes beyond" what simply is toward what can be: the factual... always emerges in light of the possible, where the possible is... a function of the agent's *choice* and *decision*.[177]

Existence, of course, consists of both facticity and transcendence in existentialism. What a particular agent chooses as a mode of life is critical for the existentialist. Transcendence always brings a sense of estrangement, which for existentialism is alienation.

Alienation results in the self's awareness that the self is estranged from self and from the world. The self understands that in creating oneself, the world takes on meaning; but the world, in the process, stands over and against the self as "an other." If the self is engaged in creating meaning for self, the world is alien to self. I am no longer a piece in a well-ordered universe, but at odds with the forces that attempt to shape my reality. The world consists of other people, and as such, forces me to see myself as the world of people see me. The tension of "being for self," and "being for others" creates alienation.

Existentialism insists that the alienation discussed here is due to the belief that choice-making, in a world of people, results in having to see one's self from "an other's" perspective. Self is constantly confronted with a world perspective of what a proper self should be. Holding fast to our choices against the world's perspective gives rise to a feeling of, in the words of the slave song, "This world is not my home and I can't feel at home, here, anymore."[178]

Existentialism insists that the self's alienation from self constitutes the constant situation of having to choose living *pour soi* in the face of pressure to choose living *en soi*. In the process of creating being, self realizes that self is constantly transforming and evolving. No permanent self remains, only self in creation given the constant emergence of new arenas of decision-making. Self is always tempted to fix a self in a changing world of choices. Such a submission to a fixed self is a form of bad faith.

Authenticity, for existentialism, is an attitude of commitment to self- making in spite of the alienation felt by the subject:

> Thus, the norm of authenticity refers to a kind of "transparency" with regard to my situation, a recognition that I am a being who *can* be responsible for who I am. In choosing in light of this norm I can be said to recover myself from alienation.... Authenticity... indicates a certain kind of integrity – not that of a pre-given whole... but that of a project to which I can either commit myself (and thus "become" what it entails) or else simply occupy for a time, inauthentically drifting in and out of various affairs.[179]

Again, choice lies at the door of individual authentic being. A commitment to self-creation and the exercise of freedom resolutely characterizes the authentic existence for existentialism. Some existentialists suggest that authentic existence produces a narrative of life. This point is important as we examine race as an existential process, particularly for Lewis Gordon. The narrative reveals the integrity of a whole life lived with authentic commitment. Authenticity is the sign of a subject living *pour soi.*

Existentialism is not without problems. To live an authentic existence is to face anguish, abandonment, and despair. Anguish is brought on by the realization of the responsibility of choice. Only the subject is responsible for choices made. Sartre states that through such a realization, the subject is acutely aware that she "cannot escape from the sense of complete and profound responsibility."[180]

Abandonment is the sense of knowing that no appeal can be made for the responsibility which the subject carries due to the freedom of choice. No appeal can be made to God or nature or others. The subject bears the weight of responsibility alone. Despair speaks to the range of possibilities that are at the subject's disposal. The subject has only X number of possibilities in the freedom of choice, and the subject's choosing must remain within the confines of said choices. Given this reality, the companion of freedom is despair.

Such is a short summary of the existential position. We turn our attention now to how race is an existential process.

Race and Existentialism

In this section we will analyze the primary ideas of race from an existential-phenomenological perspective. In other words, we will examine race as a matter of conscious choice. The conversation of black existential philosophy will be used, but not exclusively. Black existential philosophers address universally the concerns about race experienced by any person attempting to live an authentic existence in the context of a racialized society. Lewis R. Gordon and Frantz Fanon will be referred to as representatives of Black existential philosophy, but the thinking of Jean-Paul Sartre is also of extreme importance for this analysis as well.

Sartre is referred to often, not only because many consider him the father of French Existentialism, but also because he addressed the issue of race in many of his works. Lewis R. Gordon writes:

> Examining [race and] racism from the standpoint of
> Sartrean philosophy of existence isn't a new idea. Jean-Paul
> Sartre has explored racial concerns in some of his work of

the 1940s and 1950s, such as *Anti-Semite and Jew, Notebooks for an Ethics, The Respectful Prostitute*, "Black Orpheus," and "Black Presence." Sartre makes an effort to understand black particularity *itself from the inside.*[181]

Sartre was particularly interested in the Negritude Movement and France's problems with Algeria. Sartre considered negritude "as that which is mysterious about the black man to the white man."[182] Sartre raises a fundamental concern for blacks (i.e. all members of the African Diaspora) in the consideration of race from an existential point of view. If the fundamental existential project for Blacks is the overcoming of antiblack racism, can the overcoming of racism be accomplished without Blacks, at the same time, becoming victims of the overcoming? In other words, two fundamental problems are present when one confronts racism. Can one, while struggling against racism, avoid being racist? And, can one struggle for Black liberation without annihilating the Black race?

Gordon responds to those who suggest that the attempt to formulate a Black existential concept of race is only to recapitulate Sartrean philosophy by writing:

> It would, however, be an error to construct Africana [Black] academic existential philosophy as a fundamentally Sartrean or European based phenomenon. For although there are Africana philosophers who have been influenced by both Sartre and European thought, it would nevertheless be fallacious to assume that that influence functions as the cause instead of the opportunity. Africana philosophers already have a reason to raise existential questions of liberation and questions of identity...by virtue of racial oppression – oppression manifested most vividly in Atlantic and East Indian slave trades and the European colonization of the African continent.[183]

Fanon's influence on race as an existential phenomenological process is, for Lewis and others, unquestionable. Gordon suggests that Fanon's contribution to race as an existential process is that Fanon articulated the centrality of the "inner life" of Black experience. Writes Gordon:

The lived reality of values was needed to position the centrality of an "inner life" of black folk. This concern was also taken up by Frantz Fanon, whose search for a "postcolonial," "post-racist" society led to his articulation of the lived experience of blacks in the face of sociogenic sedimentations of their identity and political possibilities. For Fanon, blacks are locked in a situation that demands a struggle with social structures that make ethical demands on transformation futile, if not irrelevant and silly.[184]

What Fanon adds to the idea of race is placing the problem of race within the context of the structures of a given society. He elevates the existential questions of race from the individual to the social. Fanon writes:

> ... the black man's alienation is not an individual question. Beside phylogeny and ontogeny stands sociogeny... let us say that this is a question of sociodiagnostics... Man is what brings society into being. The prognosis is in the hands of those who are willing to get rid of the worm-eaten roots of the structure... any unilateral liberation is incomplete, and the gravest mistake would be to believe in their automatic interdependence.[185]

Since "existential philosophy addresses the problems of freedom, anguish, dread, responsibility, embodied agency, sociality, and liberation,"[186] it is suggested that it is the best form of philosophical examination for the matter of race.

With the existential concept of race, two fundamental questions emerge: "What are we? and, What shall we do?"[187] In other words, the questions of identity and moral action are crucial for any concept of race; existentialism brings these questions to the forefront.[188] Questions of being and action, in the light of racism, demand an examination of who we are and how we are to go on.

In examining race from the existential perspective, we must employ a descriptive ontology or existential phenomenology.[189] In employing this mode of analysis, certain assumptions are presented to us. There are five fundamental assumptions that must be understood.

1. Human beings are aware of their freedom in various situations including being a racialized subject in a race-laden society.
2. Human beings are free choosers of various aspects of their situations.
3. Human beings are responsible for their condition on some level.
4. Human beings have the power to change themselves when coming to grips with their situation.
5. There exist features of the human condition that provide rich areas of creative interpretation by human beings for the creation of personal narratives.

Articulating the power of these assumptions, Gordon writes:

> To determine what kind of a self a human being chooses as his project is to determine not only what kind of human being the chooser is, but also who the human being may be in his particularity in virtue of the choices which make his life meaningful. Hence to study an aspect of human reality is to study the mode of being or ontology of that aspect of human reality itself. [Black and other racialized] people have the misfortune of being situated in the *what* mode of being. An existential phenomenological exploration can forge the ground for the correct basis of the *who*.[190]

While Gordon's main concern in this quote is how antiblack racism constitutes bad faith, a larger issue may be teased out. If the starting point of an analysis of race is the subject and the context in which she lives, then the first question of race is, "What is race for the subject?" The struggle between facticity and transcendence emerges here. Facticity denotes the *what* I am. Transcendence propels me to the *who* I can be.

In terms of race, a society by its constructs ascribes a race to the subject. Human beings are placed in a particular race and class. The social constructs determine a person's socio-economic value within the social structure. Society can determine the amount of access one may or may not have to the structures of privilege and power. The activity of the constructs creates the social facticity of the subject.

"What I am" as a social being is determined by the social constructs that influence my lived experiences.

Science (bio-genetics) also provides the facts of *what* I am. Racially, it gives the subject the neurophysiological description of what it means to be black and human. Science establishes the weak biological connection to race. It determines morphology, susceptibility to various medical conditions, hair texture, eye color, etc.

What social constructs and science cannot do is determine the *who* one becomes within the context of lived experiences. According to existentialism, society may ascribe me as Black, but I have the freedom to determine how I am being Black and what that means as a creating subject. To accept the categories of facticity as the true subject instead of accepting the responsibility of creating the self is a form of bad faith.

Jean-Paul Sartre states, "[I]t is best to choose and to examine one determined attitude which is essential to human reality and which is such that consciousness instead of directing its negation outward turns it toward itself. This attitude, it seems to me, is bad faith."[191] I understand Sartre to say that accepting the categories of facticity (e.g. the social construct categories of race as determinant of my being) is "consciousness... directing its negation... toward itself." I negate the choices of freedom to create and, instead, rest in sociogenic and scientific categories. In other words, when S states that S is white because S is considered white, classified as white, does what all other white people do, looks white, and then accepts such constructs and descriptions as to what it means to be S, S is living in bad faith. S has adopted the racial structures imposed by social construction or science as the way of authentic living. Attitude is of key importance in this analysis.

In describing the phenomenon of bad faith, Gordon writes:

> In bad faith, I flee a displeasing truth [I create the "who" I am] for a pleasing falsehood [I am the "who" of description and construction]. I must convince myself that a falsehood is in fact true. I therefore lie to myself. I think about who I am...and I ask myself, Am I identical with these [descriptions and constructions]? To be at peace with myself, I accept [the] "what I am, which pushes to the side

the constant question of [who] I can be[come]." Myself will
always be my responsibility.[192]

In bad faith, I only become acquainted with shadows and
semblances of being. When the subject chooses to transcend the racial
categories of social construction and genetics, and take responsibility
for self-authentication, girded with the right attitude, then and only
then is the subject in the existential process of creating race for herself.
Such a process is a process of self-authentication. Gordon refers to the
self-authenticating process as freedom to "catch ourselves."

> I am a freedom. As a freedom, I seem to have nowhere to
> settle down. Wherever I land is always posed as an object to
> me and is therefore not identical with what I am. Suppose
> we pursue ourselves. To "catch" ourselves we need first to
> make ourselves.[193]

Self-authentication demands choice and the exercise of freedom.
We must choose to "pull the rug from underneath" our socially
constructed, scientifically described self, and discover that "there is
no self; there is so to speak, a perspective that is, in itself, 'nothing.'
In facing myself as 'no-thing,' I am free."[194]

The existential process of creating race for self is a process that
necessarily causes the subject to be confronted by anguish and
irony. The subject, in the process of creating an authentic racial self,
knows that it is a continuous process of making choices. Because of
the choice-making component in creating an authentic racial self,
racial existentialists state that the subject is confronted with anguish.
Gordon writes:

> ...I face a choice over the attitude I shall have toward my
> being in the world. [T]his confrontation with choice [is]
> anguish.... [A]nguish is the confrontation with the self.
> In anguish we face the fact that we are the ones who must
> make the choices that constitute our selves. In anguish,
> then, I find myself facing the situation of who and what
> I am. I discover that I constitute myself. I face my own
> freedom and my own responsibility for it. [In anguish] I
> face myself as freedom.[195]

Irony, for the existential position, is the result of holding a belief as certain, and yet realizing the truth of it is always changing given the transitional nature of the self. As a self-creating a racial self, to believe "I am Asian" is both true and ironic. Because, as a self-creating self, what is true regarding race in the subjective moment, is not true in future moments. Gordon is clear that the truth of what it means to be a racial being in every moment is relative to that moment and cannot be the end statement of the subject's project or narrative. Gordon states, "to believe – "really" – to believe is to be certain. To recognize my belief as a belief is, however, to admit a lack of certainty."[196] Thus, racial belief for the creating subject is always both true and not true, which reveals the situation of irony. Good faith, as authentic self-creating as a racial being, always confronts the subject in irony.

Bad faith results when we idealize our racial beliefs and make them the standard of being for the subject. I believe that is what Victor Anderson objects to regarding "ontological blackness."[197] When Blackness is set as a particular standard of being, the opportunity for creative being is stymied. Sartre concludes this point by stating:

> The ideal of good faith (to believe what one believes) is, like that of sincerity (to be what one is), an ideal of being-in-itself [that is, being a definite thing or object]. Every belief is a belief that falls short; one never wholly believes what one believes. ... If every belief in good faith is an impossible belief, then there is a place for every impossible belief. [198]

The impossible racial belief for the creating subject is: I am (black) by my own freedom, responsible for my choices and conscious of the fact that the beliefs which constitute my choices are both the truth and falsity of being.

Situated in the context of creating my own self as a racial being, I experience alienation. For the other people of my world, context always sees me as something that both is and is not *who* I am. Factually I am black, male, 215 pounds, etc. But subjectively, I am not the self perceived by others; for I am, in good faith, creating, evolving, and becoming the *who* I am. Since I am a social creature, and creating self constitutes rebellion against my socially ascribed being, alienation is unavoidable. Self-creation is antithetical to conforming to the social and scientific categories of being. Choice alienates the self from others' perspective of the self. Racially, one is constantly re-evaluating self for self and self for others. The constant process of re-evaluation causally adds to the alienation experienced by the subject. Because the subject is an embodied self, issues of race are pertinent to the description of alienation.[199]

Extreme cases make this experience of alienation obvious. In slavery, the slave had to assert internally what and who he was, given the context of oppression. The slave-master, the other, gave one perspective: The slave is less than human, beast of burden, economic means to an end, etc. The other slaves gave a perspective: friend, foe, Uncle Tom, rebel, etc. In creating self for self, the slave had to constantly evaluative *what* he was and *who* he was in compliance with the perspective of others (bad faith) or creating a self in the midst of dehumanizing dynamics.

One may argue that I am only describing life in the extreme and that in the contemporary era in U.S. society I have overstated the case. But it is clear that for the existential position, the attempt to create an authentic self in the current socio-political arena is only different by degree. The existential philosophers suggest that self in relationship to others constantly is creating and re-creating self in the context of others' perspective, whether it is racial stereotypes, socially constructed racial ascriptions, or scientific taxonomies. In re-creating a racial self, one separates from the perspective of others in order to construct the psychological, historical, biographical self. The separation is in fact alienation, for the self can no longer rest in the perspectives of the other, but must – in freedom – choose the creative process for the sake of authentic living.

Perhaps the most arresting case in contemporary society is the case of Rachel Dolezal. Ms. Dolezal, born Anglo American, claimed to be an African American woman. She claims that she thinks of herself as African American and refuses to identify herself as "white." Much furor arose from every corner of American society regarding Ms. Dolezal's racial self-identification. The question that is compelling for us to ask is, can a person exercise his/her existential right to affirm a racial identity contrary to social constructural and essential rules? The case of Rachel Dolezal affirms the position that race is a matter of existential choice and a process of self-creation.

W.E.B. Du Bois articulates this phenomenon of self-creation and subsequent otherness in *The Souls of Black Folks.* In "Of Our Spiritual Strivings," Du Bois poignantly points to the attempt to be both American and African as constituting "two souls trapped in one dark body."[200] Existentialists point to Du Bois' statement as the fact that this "two-ness" is the result of having to see oneself through another's eyes *and* through one's own eyes. The two-ness is the alienation of self for self.

So, what is race for the existential phenomenological process? Race is the result of a subject knowing self as freedom, exercising the choice to continuously create in the face of irony, anguish and alienation. An existential racial identity is always confronted with the temptation of facticity, but in good faith engaging a transcending mode of being. In other words, I create who I am as a racial being if I am to live an authentic existence. Bad faith results when I allow the social constructs or scientific descriptions to determine not only *what* I am (facticity) but *who* I am. Good faith racially demands the will to create a self despite the dynamics to conform to a social ontological ascription or a genetic description. It is an exercise of will because the self is aware of resulting alienation from others, epistemological irony, and the burden of being solely responsible for choices – anguish.

While in many respects I believe this account of race is on target, there are some problems with this concept of race that cannot be overlooked. While there can be no denying that an aspect of race is existential, the position raises some interesting problems. By making race ultimately a matter of subjective choice, race can become a form of fickle racial identification.

For example, according to the existential position, there is no reason I cannot be white Bavarian German, if I am willing to see myself as freedom, exercise choice, and withstand alienation, irony, and anguish. Taken to its logical conclusion, race is solely subjective. But if that is true, anyone can be any race at any subjective moment, if they so choose. But if anyone can be any race, then there is no such thing as race. Clearly such a conclusion is counter-productive to the quest of defining race.

Thus, the Rachel Dolezal case and cases of the *passing* phenomenon are problematic. We understand *passing* by people of color as a means to access privilege of the dominant Anglo culture, but it is confusing to us that a member of a privileged group would willfully *pass* to an under-privileged group. We are fascinated by films where the character immerses into another racial/cultural group to the point that the character sees herself as completely a member of said group. Dustin Hoffman in "*Little Big Man*" and Tom Cruise in "*The Last Samurai*" prove the point. But we are outraged when this event happens in real life. The amount of negative reaction to Rachel Dolezal was overwhelming. My aunt and others like her, who engaged in *passing* and were discovered, experienced crushing denunciation from family, the African American community, and the dominant Anglo society.

The existential argument could be that one cannot change the factual (i.e. facticity) realities of being. Freedom, as an embodied self, is in the context of my life realities. If transcendence is a necessary component of race, why can I not transcend my African American facticity and subjectively be German? Bi-racials in the American context have made this point frequently. They emphatically state that they are not one race or the other, but both and neither. What they are is what they claim. The identity of bi-racial people is not determined by others but is an expression of their existential choice.

In the act of *passing*, one could make the argument from the existential perspective, that the self that *passes* is merely transcending the factual, and subjectively being whatever racialized person they wish to be. If truth is subjective, then the Asian that *passes* for white is really living authentically. We are then returned to the fundamental question: is race simply subjective, or are other social and scientific factors also in play? The answer is not clear.

There is a second problem at hand. The racial existential position states that authentic racial identity is a self-creative process. The onus of being is left with my creating a (racial) self for self. And so, I must constantly engage in creating and recreating, and then creating again; for to remain at one point in the creative process is to fix a self, which in turn is inauthentic living, or bad faith. In one aspect, the existentialists are right. For example, creating what it means to be black is a constant self-evaluating, self-actualizing effort. There is no such thing as a generic black person. No stereotype fits. Therefore, *how* I am *who* I am becomes my narrative for others as being Black.

But to say this poses another problem. If the existentialist is correct, what if, as a self-creating being, I choose to actualize my blackness by denying blackness all together? If my self-project is to be a narrative for others, then my narrative reads: To be Black is not to be Black. I do not see how the existentialist can get out of this obvious incongruency. If I am freedom, I choose what is "truth." If choices are a narrative of creative being, then we find ourselves trapped in this circle.

The problems above rest in the notion that racial truth is subjective. If the self is the only one who can both know and live authentically, how can we suggest that the above thought-problems are not authentic subjective modes of self creating self. Even Kierkegaard, I suggest, could answer the question of how one distinguishes between the authentic knight of faith and the inauthentic madman. Only God, for Kierkegaard, would know. But to go to heaven to find out is asking to go too far. In the case of Sartre, to inquire with God is a violation of human freedom and to accept the socially constructed notions is to live in bad faith; therefore, there is no way to distinguish an inauthentic racial identity from an authentic one. Subjectivity leaves us with no objective criteria for evaluation and thus no way to authenticate *pour soi* racial being over and against *en soi* being. Because of our inability to distinguish authentic racial self-creating, we must reject the existential concept of race.

I offer one final objection that is more descriptive in nature. For existentialism to suggest that all of us have the power to change ourselves amid our situations is to fail to properly appreciate the power of social situations. Social constructions not only tell us who we are, they tell us how to think about who we are. This point Mills and Taylor are correct about. We are products of the constructs in which we live. One must agree that in the context of lived experiences we have the options of choosing *how* we will be, but we also must give credence to the awesome power of social constructs. To say that I absolutely choose how to be a particular racial identity is not only in volition of the rules the social constructs place in our lives, but it is also a denial of the history of the construct under which I live. My choices are shaped by the social constructs that influence life. I think existentialism fails to adequately acknowledge the power of constructs and for this reason also, we reject the existential concept of race.

The Postlude

Throughout this project, we have examined four main concepts of race. These are not the only concepts of race. For example, philosophers Dr. John McClendon, III and Dr. Stephen Ferguson suggest that race is the result of class struggle and to overcome racism one must be cognizant of the material conditions that contribute to racism as a social phenomenon. My research has not equipped me to address this idea sufficiently, but I raise it in order acknowledge that other ideas about race are on the table for discussion.

Two fundamental ideas have driven this work: 1) While we are constantly engaged in racial conversations and thinking, our conversations are disjointed and conflicting because we are not clear as to what we mean by "race;" and, 2) that it is possible to talk about "race" without talking about "racism" per se. I define racism as *a body of knowledge concerning the nature of race.* One can quickly see that each of the concepts of race discussed in the project provide a body of knowledge concerning race that either help to dismantle or promote negative racism in America. My hope is that this project will encourage dialogue about race. What we think about race has influenced every arena of our lives. It determines politics, religion, academia, business, and scientific research. All intrapersonal circles are influenced by race. Race is one of the most important and pertinent conversations we need to have if we are truly going to be the society we dream to be.

I also hope that this project increases your understanding regarding race. There is a Black jazz song that states, "Understanding is the best thing in the world." In the aftermath of Ferguson and Charlottesville (just to name two events), the need for greater understanding is apparent. This work is not a normative project, it is a descriptive one. It is not my intention to tell us how we ought to think about race, rather it is a work to describe how we think about race in the American context. All of us can think of individuals that fit one of concepts of race presented. What is most problematic is that many people attempt to mix and match the concepts which increases the muddling of racial discourse.

In the next project I will address racism in America. Suffice it to be said at this point that racism is a three-tiered phenomenon. It is experienced on the personal/individual level. This is a fact with which we are all acquainted. But racism is also institutional and systemic. It is the second and third levels of racism that are most destructive to the life of Black people and American society. It is at the second and third levels that racism is attached to privilege and power. Subsequently, in the next project, I will address the connection of racism and economics. Racial disparity and economic disparity go hand in hand.

May your personal work in dismantling racism be encouraged by this project.

Endnotes

1   Paul C. Taylor, *Race: A Philosophical Introduction*. Polity Press: Cambridge. Taylor uses this phrase throughout the book. The first place is found on page 7.

2   Robert Bernasconi and Tommy Lott, eds, *Idea of Race*. Hackett Publishing Company: Indianapolis, 2000, introduction.

3   G.W.F. Hegel, Phenomenology of Spirit,

4   Taylor, *Race: A Philosophical Introduction, pp 3-4*

5   Ibid. p.5

6   Claude McKay, The Negro's Tragedy," Stanza 1, from *Black Voices,* Abraham Chapman, ed., New American Library: New York, p. 373

7   Taylor, *Race: A Philosophical Introduction*, p 5.

8   From Internet Encyclopedia of Philosophy-Race.

9   Ibid.

10   Ibid.

11   Ibid.

12   Ibid.

13   Bernasconi and Lott, *Idea of Race*, p ix

14   This fact is commonly affirmed among scholars in the field. For a more detailed discussion of this historical event see Michael Banton's *Racial Theories.* Cambridge: Cambridge University Press, 1987.

15   Taylor, *Race: A Philosophical Introduction.* p. 41.

16   For an in-depth discussion of this idea, see Daniel Mannix and Malcolm Cowley, *Black Cargoes.* New York: Viking Press, 1962.

17   Ibid. pp. 41, 42.

18   Ibid.

19   Ibid

20   Ibid

21   *Idea of Race*, p. viii.

22   I borrow the term *Folk psychology* from the metaphysical physicalists who roughly define it as a worldview absent of scientific justification.

23   Bernasconi and Lott, *Idea of Race*. p. vii.

24   Taylor, *Race: A Philosophical Introduction*, p. 44

25   Thomas Jefferson, *Notes on the State of Virginia Writings*. New York: Liberty of America, 1984. pp. 268-269.

26   Richard H. Popkin, *Isaac La Peyere (1596-1676): His Life, Work, and Influence*. Leiden: E.J. Brill, 1987. p. 27

27   Bernasconi and Lott, *Idea of Race*, p vii.

28   Taylor, *Race: A Philosophical Introduction*, p. 44. See also, "The Color of Reason: The Idea of Race in Kant's Anthropology" in *Postcolonial African Philosophy*, Emmanuel Eze, ed. Oxford: Blackwell. 1997. pp. 103-140.

29   *Idea of Race*, p.viii

30   Kant, "Of the Different Human Races" p.8

31   Ibid

32   Ibid

33   Ibid

34   Ibid, p 10

35   Ibid

36   *Idea of Race*, p. vii

37   *Race: A Philosophical Introduction, p.43*

38   M. Nei and A. K. Roychouhury," Evolutionary Relationships of Human Population on a Global Scale." t**est.scripts.psu.edu/nxm2/1993 Public ations/1993**-nei-roychoudhury**.pdf**

39   Herder, *Ideas on the Philosophy of the history of Humankind*, p.23

40   Ibid.

41   Ibid.

42   This is borrowed from Leszek Kolakowski's book *Metaphysical Horror*. I am simply stating that the end result (though in another context) would be exactly what Kolakowski calls "metaphysical horror."

43   Ibid, p. 22

44   Ibid, p.23

45   "Modern History Sourcebook: Johann Gottfried von Herder: Materials for the Philosophy of the History of Mankind, 1784" www.fordham.edu/ ha lsall/mod/1784herder-mankind.html, p.1

46   *Idea of Race*, p viii

47   Ibid.

48   G. W. F. Hegel, "Anthropology", p.39

49   Ibid. p. 40

50   Ibid. p.41

51   Ibid.

52   *Race: A Philosophical Introduction*, p. 49

53   I have simply taken Lawarence E, Cahoone's argument on Habermas to the next level. See "Buchler on Habermas on Modernity," in *The Southern Journal of Philosophy* (1989), Vol. XXVII, No. 4.

54   I am only speaking here of evaluating X in the actual world attempting to avoid the obvious modal/temporal problems, arguments for/or against Kaplan's rigidity versus Kripke's rigidity, and the issue of tokening and other possible worlds.

55   This idea regarding European history and the formation of race as a philosophical and socio-political concept is also affirmed within the disciplines of the social sciences. The influence of Western European Anglo-American thought in connection to the conceptualization of race I argue is undeniable.

56   This idea regarding European history and the formation of race as a philosophical and socio-political

57   *Stanford Philosophical Encyclopedia, "Essentialism."* www.stanfordphiloso phicalencyclopedia.com

58   This my own exposition of the Platonic idea.

59   Naomi Zack, "Race and Philosophical Meaning," in *Newsletter on Philosophy and the Black Experience*, 1994, APA Newsletters, Spring 2000, Volume 99, Number 2. p. 2

60   Ibid. p. 1

61   Ibid. p. 1-2

62   Internet Encyclopedia of Philosophy under "Race," pp.2-3.

63   Paul C. Taylor, *Race: A Philosophical Introduction*, Cambridge: Polity Press, 2004, pp. 38-48.

64   Ibid. pp. 43, 44.

65   G. W. F. Hegel, "Anthropology," *Encyclopedia of the Philosophical Sciences*, 1830, from *The Idea of Race*, Robert Bernasconi and Tommy Lott, eds. Indianapolis: Hackett Publishing, Inc., p. 41.

66   Zack, "Race and Philosophical Meaning." p. 2

67   Kwame Anthony Appiah, *In My Father's House: Africa in the Philosophy of Culture*. New York: Oxford University Press. pp.13-15.

68   Ibid.

69   Ibid.

70   Ibid.

71   Ibid.

72   Taylor, *Race: A Philosophical Introduction*, p. 44. Also see, bell hooks,

Yearning, Race, Gender, and Cultural Politics. Boston: South End Press, 1996.

[73] Ibid.

[74] Taylor, *Race: A Philosophical Introduction.* pp. 84-87. I have stated this in the positive even though Taylor states the position in the negative.

[75] Axel R. Schafer, "W.E.B. Du Bois, German Social Thought, and the Racial Divide in American Progressivism, 1892-1909," in *Journal of American History,* Vol. 88, No 3, December 2001, p.6, 9, 11.

[76] W.E.B. Du Bois, "the Conservation of Races," pp.73-76

[77] Ibid.

[78] Appiah, *In My Father's House,* p. 29

[79] Du Bois, The Conservation of Races, p. 77

[80] Ibid.

[81] This point has been made by Cornel West in his reading of Du Bois, particularly in Du Bois' *The Souls of Black Folks.*

[82] M. Nei, "Evolution of human races at the gene level." https://**www.ncbi.nlm.nih.gov**/pubmed/7163193 and, M. Nei and A. K. Roychouhury, "Genic variation within and between the three major races of man, Caucasoids, Negroids, and Mongoloids.". https://**www.ncbi.nlm.nih.gov**/pubmed/4841634.

[83] Appiah, *In My Father's House,* p. 38

[84] Ibid. p.39

[85] Ibid.

[86] This line of thinking is a recapitulation of Gilbert Ryle. And

[87] Taylor, *Race,* p. 86

[88] This is the classic statement from Gilbert Ryle with a twist. Ryle's argument against Cartesian dualism seems appropriate here. For more on Ryle and his objections to "the official doctrine" (i.e. Dualism) see Gilbert Ryle, *The Concept of Mind.* Chicago: University of Chicago Press, 1949.

[89] Sally Haslanger. "Gender and Race: (What) Are They? (What) Do We Want Them To Be?" *Nous* (March 2000): 11+. Online. MSN. 16 May 2005. www.mit.edu/~shaslang/papers/WIGRnous.pdf.

[90] All the resources explored for this project confirm this fact. An example of this position can be found in Zack, Naomi. "American Mixed Race: The U.S. 2000 Census and Related Issues." Interracial Voice. 9 Dec.2004:1. http://www.interracialvoice.com/zack.html

[91] Definition from "Social Construction." 16 December 2005: 1. http://plato.stanford.edu/entries/social-construction/ .

[92] I get this from readings in social constructionism. I refer you to the following as a good exposition of this type of thinking. Peter L. Berger and Thomas Luckman. *The Social Construction of Reality.* New York:

Doubleday Publishing Co. 1966.

[93] Ibid. p. 2

[94] Ibid.

[95] Ibid.

[96] Ibid.

[97] Hacking, Ian. *The Social Construction of What?* Cambridge: Harvard University Press: 2001. p. 29-30.

[98] Taylor, Paul. *Race: A Philosophical Introduction*, Cambridge: Polity Press 2004, p. 84.

[99] Ibid. p. 84-85

[100] Mills, Charles W. "But What Are You Really?" in *Blackness Visible: Essays on Philosophy and Race*. Ithaca: Cornell University Press 1998. p. 44-50.

[101] Ibid. p. 45.

[102] Ibid.

[103] Ibid. Mills interchangeably uses the terms ontology and metaphysics.

[104] Ibid.

[105] Ibid.

[106] Ibid. pp.45-46.

[107] Ibid. p. 48

[108] Ibid. p.44-45

[109] Taylor, Paul. *Race: A Philosophical Introduction*, p. 86, 88, 91.

[110] Ibid. p. 91.

[111] Ibid.

[112] Mills, Charles W. "But What Are You Really." p. 48.

[113] I became formally aware of this problem from two main sources. The first was in reading Charles H. Mills, "But What Are You Really? The Metaphysics of Race," Problem Case II, *Blackness Visible: Essays on Philosophy and Race*. Ithaca: Cornell University Press: 1998. p 56-57. It is clear that the problem of "passing" is major for other philosophers as well. Also, see Walter Benn Michaels, "Race Into Culture: A Critical Genealogy of Cultural Identity," Critical Inquiry 18, 1992: p. 655-687; and, Ron Mallon, "Passing, Traveling and Reality: Social Constructionism and the Metaphysics of Race," *Nous* 38:4 2004: p. 644-673.

[114] The "Pudd'nhead Wilson Syndrome" comes from Mark Twain's literary work, *The Tragedy of Pudd'nhead Wilson*. In this work, two infants with indistinguishable features, one a black slave and the other a white heir, are switched and are raised as members of their switched races until a later date.

[115] I am referring to the case of Susie Phipps and the State of Louisiana where the State of Louisiana declared her black after years of thinking she was white. Gregory Williams found out he was black in his

adolescence when his parents divorced. Of course, one must remember that they are victims of the "one drop rule."

[116] This is merely a psycho-historical claim. It is one that is intuitively true and, in most cases, historically evidenced. It is not an appeal to the necessary and sufficient causes (conditions) of *passing*, which are material, given a social constructionist context. The necessary and sufficient causes are: alienation, oppression, class and social difference, the inequality of economic distribution, death, etc. The psychological causes are less clear.

[117] Mallon, Ron. "Passing, Traveling and Reality: Social Constructionism and The Metaphysics of Race." p. 648.

[118] I have added this to the constraints because it seems to me that if a concept is to do its work, it ought to lay out categorical phenomena that are permissible and impermissible. If the claim is that, as a social construct, all activity, cognitive and social, is prescribed by the construct, then all actions within its parameters are permissible; those outside are not permissible.

[119] Michaels, Walter Benn. "Race into Culture: A Critical Genealogy of Cultural Identity." Critical Inquiry 18: 1992. p. 655-685.

[120] Ibid. p. 768-769.

[121] Ibid. p. 758

[122] This term comes from Mallon and seems to be the consistent labeling of Michaels first argument in all the literature. This argument is laid out in the previously cited article by Mallon.

[123] Mallon, "Passing, Traveling and Reality:" pp. 649-650

[124] Ibid. p.649

[125] Ibid.

[126] Ibid. p. 652

[127] Mills, "But What Are You Really?" p.50

[128] Ibid. p. 50-54.

[129] Mallon, p.652

[130] Ibid. p.653

[131] Ibid.

[132] Mills, p.51

[133] Taylor, Paul C. *Race: A Philosophical Introduction.* p. 101

[134] From Ronald R. Sundstrom, "Racial Nominalism" in *Journal of Social Philosophy*, Volume 33, No 2, Summer 2002, p.194

[135] Mills, Charles, "But What Are You Really? The Metaphysics of Race." In *Blackness Visible: Essays on Race and Philosophy*. Ithaca: Cornell University Press, 1998, p. 50.

[136] Taylor, Paul C. *Race: A Philosophical Introduction,* Cambridge: Polity Press, 2004 p. 87.

[137] Sean Thomas, The London Sunday Telegraph, 3/13/05. From Alan

Goodman, "Two Questions About Race, *Is Race "Real"?* Social Science Research Council. 2005. http://raceandgenomics.ssrc.org/ Goodman/

138 John Shuford, "Four Du Boisian Contributions to Critical Race Theory," presented to The Society for the Advancement of American Philosophy, 28th Annual Meeting, March 11-13, 2001. http://www.americanphilosophy. org/archives/2001%20Conference/Discussion%20papers/shuford

139 This critique can be found in numerous places within the literature. I suggest two readings that stress this point. See Debra J. Dickerson, *The End of Blackness,* New York: Pantheon Books, 2004; and, Victor Anderson, *Beyond Ontological Blackness,* New York: Orbis Books, 1999.

140 Ibid. p.3.

141 Ibid. p.35 and 36.

142 Ibid. p. 37.

143 Ibid.

144 Ibid.

145 Appiah, Kwame Anthony. "The Uncompleted Argument: Du Bois and the Illusion of Race." In *Race, Class, Gender, and Sexuality: The Big Questions.* Edited by Naomi Zack, Laurie Shrage, and Crispin Sartwell. Maden: Blackwell Publishing, Inc., 1999, p. 83.

146 Appiah, p. 36, found in Ronald R. Sundstrom, "Racial Nominalism," *Journal of Social Philosophy,* Vol. 33, Number 2, Summer 2002, Maden: Blackwell Publishing, Inc., 2002, p.194.

147 Taylor, Paul. *Race: A Philosophical Introduction,* Cambridge: Polity Press 2004, p. 67.

148 Ibid. p.86

149 Jones, D. Marvin. "A Darkness Made Visible: Law, Metaphor, and the Racial Self." In *Critical White Studies: Looking Behind the Mirror.* Edited by Richard Delgado and Jean Stefanic, Philadelphia: Temple University Press, 1997, p 67.

150 Zack, Naomi. "American Mixed Race: The U.S. 200 Census and Related Issues." *Interracial Voice, http://www.interracialvoice.com/zack.html*

151 Zack, Naomi. *Race and Mixed Race.* Philadelphia: Temple University Press, 1993, p. 3-4.

152 Shuford. p. 4

153 See Ronald R. Sundstrom, "Racial" Nominalism," pp. 195-196.

154 This argument is taken from John Shuford's "Four DuBoisian Contributions to Critical Race Theory," p.4.

155 Zack, Naomi. "An Autobiographical View of Mixed Race and Deracination." 91 APA Newsletters, 1, (Spring, 1992), p. 10.

156 Burroughs, Valentine J., Maxey, Randell W., Levy, Richard A., "Racial and Ethnic Differences in Response to Medicines: Towards Individualized Pharmaceutical Treatment," *Journal of the National Medical Association,*

Vol. 94, NO 10 (Supplemental), October 2002, p. 8.

[157] The information regarding bio-racial drugs comes from the National Marrow Donation Program. See nmdpresearch.org.

[158] Ibid.

[159] The literature in Critical Race Theory is replete with this argument. I will point out two. See Charles W. Mills, "Revisionists Ontologies: Theorizing White Supremacy, *Blackness Visible: Essays on Philosophy and Race,* Ithaca: Cornell University Press, 1998; Linda Martin-Alcoff, What Should White People Do, *Hypanthia,* Summer 98, Vol. 13, just to mention two sources.

[160] Taylor. *Race: A Philosophical Introduction,* p.126

[161] West, Cornel. *Democracy Matters,* New York: Penguin Books, 2004, p. 40-41.

[162] Quote from James Baldwin's *Many Thousand Gone,* found in Cornel West's *Democracy Matters,* p. 84.

[163] Taylor, p. 127

[164] Toni Morrison from Cornel West's *Democracy Matters,* p. 95.

[165] Howard Thurman. *America in Search for a Soul,* found in Cornel West's *Democracy Matters* New York: Penguin Books, 2004, p. 145

[166] Ron Mallon, "Passing Traveling and Reality: Social Constructionism and the Metaphysics of Race," Nous, 38:4 (2004), p. 644-673.

[167] Paraphrase of Martin Luther King's "I Have a Dream" speech given August 28, 1963.

[168] This point has become increasing popular given the recent conversations of prominent African Americans. See transcript of "the State of Black American" produced and presented by CNN, March 4, 2006. See also Cornel West, R*ace Matters*. New York: Penguin Books, 1994.

[169] Descartes. *Meditations on First Philosophy,* 3

[170] Descartes. *Meditation,* 2

[171]—Ibid. *Meditation,*5

[172] Heidegger's use of the term "dasein" in Being and Time would incorporate one's awareness of racial identity.

[173] Aristotle. *Metaphysics* [1031a-1031b] 4-6.

[174] Samuel E. Stumpf and James Fieser. *Socrates to Sartre and Beyond: A History of Philosophy, Seventh Edition,* New York: McGraw-Hill Publishing, 2003 p.359

[175] Jean Paul Sartre. *Existentialism is a Humanism,* found in *Philosophical Issues and Problems, Second Edition,* Joseph Bien and William Bondeson, Boston: Pearson Custom Publishing, 2000. p. 90.

[176] *Stanford Encyclopedia of Philosophy, "Existentialism"* by Steven Crowell, 2004, p.7 http://plato. stanford.edu/entries/existentialism 3/6/2006.

[177] Ibid. p.8

[178] This song was sung often in my home by my grandmother who was born in slavery. The origin I do not know. However, it was a song known by others of her generation and was sung regularly in my home church.

[179] *Stanford Encyclopedia of Philosophy*, *"Existentialism"* by Steven Crowell, 2004, p.7 http://plato. stanford.edu/entries/existentialism 3/6/2006.

[180] Jean-Paul Sartre. "Existentialism is a Humanism" in *Existentialism from Dostoyevsky to Sartre*, ed. Walter Kaufman, Liverpool: Meridian Publishing Company, 1989. http://www.marxists.org/reference/ archive/sartre/ works/exist/sartre.htm 3/6/2006

[181] Lewis R. Gordon. *Bad Faith and Antiblack Racism*. Amherst: Humanity Books, 1999 p. 3

[182] Gordon, p. 3

[183] Lewis R. Gordon. *Existentia Africana*. New York: Routledge, 2000. p. 9.

[184] Gordon. *Existentia Africana*, p. 4.

[185] Frantz Fanon. *Black Skin, White Masks*. Grove Press, 1967 p.11

[186] Gordon. *Existentia Africana*, p. 7

[187] Gordon, Existentia Africana, p.7

[188] Ibid.

[189] Gordon, *Bad Faith and Antiblack Racism*, p. 5

[190] Gordon, *Bad faith and Antiblack Racism*, p.6

[191] Jean-Paul Sartre. *Being and Nothingness: A Phenomenological Essay on Ontolog*, translated with introduction by Hazel Barnes. New York: Washington Square Press, 1956. p.87

[192] Gordon, *Bad Faith and Antiblack Racism*, p. 8-9

[193] Gordon, p. 9.

[194] Ibid.

[195] Gordon, p.13-14.

[196] Gordon, p.11

[197] See the elaboration of this idea in Victor Anderson's *Beyond Ontological Blackness: An Essay on African American Religious and Cultural Criticism*. New York: Continuum, 1995.

[198] Quote from Jean-Paul Sartre found in Lewis R. Gordon's *Bad Faith and Antiblack Racism*, p.11-12.

[199] Lewis R. Gordon. *Bad Faith and Antiblack Racism*, p. 44.

[200] W.E.B. Du Bois. *The Souls of Black Folks*, published 1903, republished New York: Fawcett Publications, Inc., 1961.